Curriculum Vitae

ALSO BY MURIEL SPARK

Curriculum Vitae

AUTOBIOGRAPHY

MURIEL SPARK

Houghton Mifflin Company
Boston   New York
1993

For information about permission to reproduce selections from this book, write
to Permissions, Houghton Mifflin Company, 215 Park Avenue South,
New York, New York 10003.

Portions of this book originally
appeared in *The New Yorker*.

Library of Congress Cataloging-in-Publication Data
Spark, Muriel.
Curriculum vitae : autobiography / Muriel Spark.
p.   cm.
ISBN 0-395-65372-X
1. Spark, Muriel—Biography.   2. Novelists, Scottish—20th
century—Biography.   I. Title.
PR6037.P29Z463   1993
823'.914—DC20
[B]   92-31270
CIP

Printed in the United States of America

BP   10 9 8 7 6 5 4 3 2 1

CONTENTS

ILLUSTRATIONS

INTRODUCTION

I am a hoarder of two things: documents and trusted friends. The former outweigh the latter in quantity but the latter outdo the former in quality.

Details fascinate me. I love to pile up details. They create an atmosphere. Names, too, have a magic, be they never so humble. Most of the names in this, the following account of the first thirty-nine years of my life, are unknown to the public. For that very reason they are all the more precious to me.

So many strange and erroneous accounts of parts of my life have been written since I became well known, that I felt it time to put the record straight.

I determined to write nothing that cannot be supported by documentary evidence or by eyewitnesses; I have not relied on my memory alone, vivid though it is. The disturbing thing about false and erroneous statements is that well-meaning scholars tend to repeat each other. Lies are like fleas hopping from here to there, sucking the blood of the intellect. In my case, the truth is often less flattering, less romantic, but often more interesting than the false story. Truth by itself is neutral and has its own dear beauty; especially in a work of non-fiction it is to be cherished. Besides, false data lead to false premises and those to false conclusions. Is it fair to scholars and students of literature to let them be misled even on the most insignificant matters? One writer of a recent biography, having given a false account of me on a demonstrably non-existent occasion, expressed herself puzzled at my objection. Her scenario showed me in what she conceived a 'good' light. Be that as it might, it was all untrue. It showed me to be a flourishing hostess at a time when I was little known and poor. (And one does not want one's early poverty mocked.) It showed me to have among my 'guests' two notable people who at that time I did not know. What was damaging about the lie, the biographer wanted to know. Damaging! Slices of three people's biographies are falsified, mine and two others. But far worse than personal damage is the damage done to truth and to scholarship.

The above is only one example of irresponsible reportage; it can only confound literary history. I am sure that many of the life-stories of my successful colleagues suffer equally.

For the memories of my early youth my best source of confirmation and information is my brother Philip Camberg who, being five and a half years my elder, has been able to recall names, places, dates, facts, more clearly than I could. (A childhood memory from the age of four can obviously be more clearly realized when the same knowledge and experience were shared with a child of nine and a half.) My brother, now a retired research chemist in the United States, entered into the checking of my childhood memories with the greatest enthusiasm.

My cousin Violet Caro also helped to confirm my young memories, and my young cousin Martin Uezzell has been to a great deal of trouble to look up and unearth family details. My son Robin Spark has looked out for me some of our family photographs to enrich the supply sent to me by my brother Philip.

When a version of my childhood experiences first appeared in the *New Yorker* I was delighted by the number of people who wrote to me to confirm, modify and elaborate on what I had written. These were either eyewitness contemporaries or their children. One of my warmest correspondents is Barbara Below, daughter of the 'Professor Rule', a friend of my parents, who captured my imagination between the ages of three and four, and whose wife Charlotte taught me to read and write. Mrs Below has gone to endless trouble to identify incidents and dates, and obtain for me the charming photograph of Charlotte Rule reproduced in this book.

And what would I have done for my Edinburgh school-days without the help of my friend Ian Barr and that of my schoolmates? Ian Barr, now retired, is a scholar and thinker with great attributes of warmth and entertainment-power; he has been indefatigable in producing data from difficult sources of information for me. Ian Barr, in the true Scottish style, was a young man in the Post Office before he rose to be Chairman of the Post Office Board; so many years later he still remembered my parents' address in Edinburgh where telegrams and special messages were delivered. And my schoolmates; Frances Niven (now Cowell), my best friend of those years, has helped me throughout, not merely with corroborative facts but with the encouragement of an old and affectionate friendship. I am grateful to Cathie Davie (now Semeonoff) who has given me her invaluable memories of Bruntsfield Links as it was when we walked across it in our youth. I warmly thank Elizabeth Vance whose letters have amused and sustained me and whose vivid impressions of our life at James Gillespie's School I have quoted from. Also for anecdotal reminiscences and amusing recollections about our school-days I thank Dorothy Forrester and Dorothy Forrest (now Rankine).

It is from the 1940s onward that I possess the greatest bulk of letters and other documents, and for her care of and deep interest in these archives over the past twenty-four years I express my gratitude to my constant supporter and companion, Penelope Jardine. It is thanks to her intelligent listing and docketing that I am able to lay hands on the papers required both to stimulate and verify my thoughts of the past. It is thanks to her sense of humour that I have enjoyed what at first looked like an alarming task. And it is Penelope Jardine to whom I owe gratitude for the use of rooms in her capacious house where she has stacked, arranged and accommodated this accumulation of papers.

The present memoir brings me up to early 1957, when I published my first novel. There are few famous names in this period of my life, but it was indeed full and rich. I hope to have given a picture of my formation as a creative writer.

I used to have an elderly friend in Rome, Lady Berkeley (Molly) whom I would sometimes visit in her flat in the Palazzo Borghese. Molly lived in style. When I asked her about the past, which she loved to talk about, she would send the butler for her book of family memoirs to check the facts. I thought it an excellent idea. Perhaps we should all write down our reminiscences to keep us from straying from reality in our latter days.

I have frequently written autobiographical pieces. What I have felt when composing them, and what I have experienced throughout my work on this volume, is a sense of enriched self-knowledge. 'Who am I?' is always a question for poets. I once had a play commissioned in the early days of my vocation. I met the producer for the first time one night to hand over the first act. Next day I received a wire: 'Darling this is what we were hoping for. Ring me at ten a.m. tomorrow, darling.' I duly phoned him at ten the next morning and gave the secretary my name. He came on the phone. I repeated my name. 'Who are you, darling?' he said.

I thought it a very good question, and still do. I resolved, all those years ago, to write an autobiography which would help to explain, to myself and others: Who am I.

I owe special acknowledgement to *The New Yorker* magazine in whose pages a number of the following chapters appeared.

In addition to those of my friends and relations mentioned above, to whom I have expressed my indebtedness, I would like to thank the following people and institutions both for their useful volunteered information and for their unfailingly cheerful responsiveness to my questions:

The Hon. Peter Acton; The British Council, Rome; The

British Institute, Florence; Mr Robert L. Bates; Mr Alan S. Bell, Rhodes House Library; Mr Nigel Billen; Mr Terence C. Charman, The Imperial War Museum, London; Mr Bill Denholm; Mr John Dunlap, Royal Mail, Edinburgh; Ms Mary Durham; Mr Tom Erhardt, Casarotto Ramsay Ltd; Mr Howard Gerwing, University of Victoria Library, BC; Prof. John Glavin; Mr Chris Green, The Poetry Society, London; Ms Jean Guild; Ms Cathy Henderson and Ms Sally Leach of the Harry Ransom Research Library, University of Texas at Austin; Mr Hardwicke Holderness; Mr Peter Hutcheon; Judge Don W. Kennedy; Prof. D.R.B. Kimbell, Faculty of Music, University of Edinburgh; The Merchant Company of Edinburgh; Mr Charles McGrath and the Checkers of *The New Yorker* magazine; The McLellan Gallery, Glasgow; Mr Michael Olver; Mr Leslie A. Perowne; Mr Terence Ranger, St Anthony's College, Oxford; Mr Kevin Ray, Washington University, St Louis, Mo.; Mr Colin Smith, Ministry of Agriculture, Fisheries and Food; Dr Jay Snyder; Mr Tony Strachan; The Hon. Guy Strutt; Mr Alan Taylor, Scotland on Sunday; M. Alain Vidal-Naquet; Mr Auberon Waugh; Mr Gerald Weiss; Mr Anthony Whittome and Ms Joan Winterkorn.

MURIEL SPARK

Oliveto, 1992

15

CHAPTER ONE

Bread, Butter and Florrie Forde

Groping for the luminous past of my first infancy I never fail to find it gleaming here and there; but never in chronological order as when I think of my later years. My childhood in Edinburgh, so far as my memory stretches back (to when I was three or four and on to my school-days) occurs in bright flashes, illuminating every detail of the scene. It would falsify the situation to try to connect my earliest years in a single narrative.

I was born in Edinburgh, at 160 Bruntsfield Place, the Morningside district, in 1918.

Bread

Bread came from Howden's, the shop above the ovens where it was made. The pavement outside the shop was warm, and hot air steamed out of a grating near the door. The floury baker and his boy (known, not unkindly, as 'the daft laddie', since he was rather simple) were white all over, the baker wore a white hat, flat at the top like an upturned pie-dish, the boy's was also flat-topped: they carried trays of bread on their heads. As they came up with their trays of bread into the shop their faces and hands, their overalls were white, and their shoes were flour-dusted.

Bread came in many forms including high pan, square pan, and cottage loaf. Of the first two you could buy a half-pan or a whole pan, according to your needs. High pan was an arch-topped rectangle, and made slices that, cut diagonally and spread with jam, were elegant for afternoon tea. Square pans were good for making up a lunch, known as a piece to take to work or school. They were also better for making breakfast toast. A cottage loaf looked like a domed chapel with a small square annexe. It looked decorative on the table.

In the morning, warm, round bappy rolls with a powdering of flour were procured from the baker, as also were bran scones, triangular and made of brown flour – virtuous, good for your health. Oat cakes, triangular biscuits, were even healthier. In the afternoon came a fresh supply of breads, sometimes Sally Lunns, embedded with currants and raisins. In Edinburgh the favourite tea-time bread was a shearer's bap, which was flat and warm. (Bapper is the Scottish word for baker.) Soda scones were generally made at home, but Howden's, too, did a brisk afternoon trade in those small, sharp-tasting lumps, thirsty for butter.

Butter

Butter came from the Buttercup Dairy Company.

A pink-and-white complexioned girl, with her hair in a cap and wearing a sparkling white overall under bright lights in winter, stood behind the marble-topped counter, beside two huge slabs of butter which reached to her shoulder. One of these slabs was fresh butter and the other was salt. Salt butter was cheaper and many people preferred it. Fresh butter was brought in from the farm every morning. The pink-and-white girl took a slice of greaseproof paper and laid it on the bright brass scales. She then took two large wooden butter-pats, one in each hand. Before she cut off your daily pound or half-pound she dipped the pats into a blue-and-white porcelain bowl of cold water. With the wooden pats she then placed each portion of butter deftly on the scales to be weighed, and she added or took away like a sculptor with his clay, until she had achieved the required weight. Now came the beautiful and clever part. The girl placed her butter, in its paper, on the counter; next, still with her pats, she cut it into cubic portions – small pieces of about a quarter of a pound – and then swiftly and neatly she worked each small cube into a flat round. Finally she took a wooden butter-stamp and, after dipping it in water, stamped each butter-medallion with a sharp slap. The imprint that was left was surrounded at the edge with the words 'Buttercup Dairy Company', and in the middle, on the butter, was the form of a small girl kneeling on one knee beside a friendly cow, under whose chin she held a buttercup. (This was a reference to our childhood custom of holding a buttercup under each other's chin with the words 'Do you like butter?' If the skin reflected a small yellow glow the answer was Yes. So far as I recall the answer was never No.) All this butter performance took place in a twinkling of an eye.

From The Buttercup, as we called the shop, we also obtained eggs of various grades. New-laid eggs were best for breakfast, but preserved eggs which had been laid down in waterglass were cheaper and perfectly adequate for cake-making. One day The Buttercup installed a fascinating egg-illuminator, on which each egg was placed before it was sold. This process, known as candling, proved the freshness of the egg. The inward egg lit up, translucent, proving the egg was good. If it had been a bad egg, it would have been opaque, but I never saw one of those.

Before leaving the shop (as, indeed, every shop), you counted your change very carefully in case of mistakes. This performance was attentively watched by the assistant who served you.

It was with the Buttercup Dairy Company that I associated Robert Louis Stevenson's lines from my earliest infancy:

One morning, very early, before the sun was up,
I rose and found the shining dew on every buttercup.

And the sparkle and morning-freshness of the shop, and the butter-conjuring girl, formed a mind-picture that accompanied the whole of my youth.

Tea

Sixty years ago is a short time in history. As recently as that I made at least one pot of tea for the family every day. It was delicious tea. Every schoolgirl, every schoolboy, knew how to make that exquisite pot of tea.

You boiled the kettle, and just before it came to the boil, you half-filled the teapot to warm it. When the kettle came to the boil, you kept it simmering while you threw out the water in the teapot and then put in a level spoonful of tea for each person and one for the pot. Up to four spoonfuls of tea from that sweetly odorous tea-caddy would make the perfect pot. The caddy spoon was a special shape, like a small silver shovel. You never took the kettle to the teapot; always the pot to the kettle, where you filled it, but never to the brim.

You let it stand, to 'draw', for three minutes.

The tea had to be drunk out of china, as thin at the rim as you could afford. Otherwise you lost the taste of the tea.

You put in milk sufficient to cloud the clear liquid, and sugar if you had a sweet tooth. Sugar or not was the only personal choice allowed.

Everyone who came to the house was offered a cup of tea, as in Dostoyevsky. What his method of making tea was I don't know. (Tea from samovars must have been different, certainly without milk, and served in a glass set in a brass or silver holder.)

Tea at five o'clock was an occasion for visitors. One ate bread and butter first, graduating to cakes and biscuits. Five o'clock tea was something you 'took'. If you had it at six you 'ate' your tea.

Tea at half-past six was high tea, a full meal which resembled breakfast. You had kippers, smoked haddock (smokies), ham, eggs or sausages for high tea. Potatoes did not accompany this meal. But a pot of tea, with bread, butter and jam, was always part of it.

Auntie Gertie and Florrie Forde

'The English' in the Edinburgh of my childhood were considered to be superficial and hypocritical. And over-dressed. My mother, who was English, used to come and fetch me from school. It was my daily dread that she should open her mouth and thus betray her suspect origins. 'Foreigners' were fairly tolerated but 'the English' were something quite different. It was not only the accent that betrayed Englishness. It was also turns of phrase and idiomatic usage. One day, outside the school, I heard my mother remark to another mother, 'I have some shopping to do.' I nearly died. She should have said, 'I've got to get the messages,' that's what she should have said. My mother also wore a winter coat trimmed with beige fox fur in the style of the then Duchess of York, now the Queen Mother (who still, and sublimely, wears those fox-trimmed coats). This was entirely out of place. My mother ought to have worn tweed or, in very cold weather, musquash. My mother wore peach-coloured silk or rayon stockings, which should have been lisle-thread, grey. It was only through her natural amiability to everyone she encountered that she managed to squeeze by the censor. She completely enjoyed meeting and greeting people. Before I was born she had been a 'teacher of pianoforte'. I still have her brass plate inscribed to that effect.

My father spoke with a strong Edinburgh accent, and although he was a Jew, having been born and educated in Edinburgh of Scottish-Jewish parents, he wore the same sort of clothes as the other fathers and spoke as they did, about the same things. So he was no problem. He was an engineer. I still have the contract of his seven-year apprenticeship signed, in schoolboy calligraphy, 'Bertie Camberg'.

'Scotch or English?' was a game played by rough boys. They would tie a stone to a length of string and whirl it around, accosting other boys with the challenge: 'Are you Scotch or English?' The invariable response was to say 'English' and run fast. The essence of the game was the ensuing chase and stone-batter. There were no real English boys involved.

Another version of the game was 'Scotch or Irish?', both harking back to what Wordsworth called,

> . . . old, unhappy, far-off things
> And battles long ago.

In an old book of memoirs (*Mary Somerville* edited by her daughter Martha Somerville, 1873) the author's mother recalls in her Scottish childhood *c.* 1788 playing a game called Scotch and English, which 'represented a raid on the debatable land, or Border between Scotland and England, in which each party tried to rob the other of their play-things. The little ones were always compelled to be English, for the bigger girls thought it too degrading.'

At home, if I left the tap running in the bathroom, my mother would say, 'Turn off the tap,' but my father's command was, 'Turn off the well.'

Taps were also wells to his young sister, my Auntie Gertie, as they were to our God-fearing neighbours. Auntie Gertie stayed with us for a while. She went out with boyfriends, dressed in a short-skirted navy blue outfit and a cherry-red hat that hugged her bobbed hair. She regarded most of her boyfriends as objects of amusement, regaling us, on her return, with pointed, merry anecdotes. Once, when she had been taken to admire a beauty spot, my auntie had remarked, in her lively way, 'Very pictureskew!' To which the boyfriend solemnly replied, 'Oh, is *that* how it's pronounced?'

We often laughed at others in our house, and I picked up the craft of being polite while people were present and laughing later if there was anything to laugh about, or criticizing later if there was anything to deplore. At this time I must have been four or five. Sometimes people got nicknames for use amongst ourselves. Like other nuggets of my early childhood, they continue to gleam in my mind, although often I forget who the people were to whom the nicknames were attached. One friend of a friend, whom my mother and I encountered sometimes at the putting green of Bruntsfield Links, was called the Ray of Sunshine. She was lodging with a couple known to my parents; the husband had assured them that this lady was 'a ray of sunshine'. In reality she looked terribly grim as she tried in a vexed way to get her golf ball into the hole. 'We met the Ray of Sunshine,' my mother merrily told my father when we got home for tea.

I had been given a dolls' pram constructed for twins, with a folding hood at each end. My dolls, Red Rosie and Queenie, sat facing each other. I remember one day I was crying and bawling for some reason. My father fetched a face-cloth and wiped the faces of my two dolls, bidding them each not to cry. I was so fascinated by this performance that I stopped crying, and I distinctly recall experiencing a sensation or instinct that, if I could have put it into words, would have been 'I'm not taken in by his ruse, but at the same time what a good child-psychologist he is!'

It must have been about 1923, just before I went to school, that I went to my first theatre show, a matinée at the Lyceum. It was surely a public holiday, for neither Auntie Gertie nor my father went to work. Instead, my parents left me in the charge of Gertie and went off in high spirits to the Musselburgh races. Presumably, my brother, five years my elder, went with them or had been sent somewhere else. Auntie Gertie and I were alone. We had our lunch, which was 'dinner' to us. She then dressed me in my best clothes and, herself looking very natty in her cherry hat and her skirt that showed her knees, conveyed me forth 'to see Florrie Forde'.

Florrie Forde was a music-hall performer. The house was packed. I had never been in a house so big, in such a big room, with so many people sitting in tiers going up and up. The curtain rose to reveal buxom Miss Forde, dressed in a one-piece suit resembling the modern body-tights, all gold-bronze spangles.

There was a thunder of applause. I was accustomed to hearing applause, because my parents used to have 'musical evenings', when my mother played, and my father sang 'Forever and Forever', or my mother herself sang 'Rose in the Bud'; on such occasions our guests would clap their hands warmly at the end of the piece. But this affair of Florrie Forde down there on the stage was so vastly public that I was full of wonder at how she could carry it all without apparently feeling shy.

She carried it off as if the stage were her own home. Other people on the stage came and went, especially men in evening dress, but Florrie in her spangles dominated the enormous house. She sang to the accompaniment of an orchestra and also danced. Only one of her numbers has remained in my memory. Miss Forde reclined glittering in the middle of the stage beside an enormous wireless set with multi-coloured, illuminated 'valves', which looked like light bulbs. Radios with valves were then a luxury in our parts. My brother had only recently constructed a wireless set that was operated by a small lump of uneven and shining metal called 'the crystal' and a wire called 'the cat's whisker'. It was a complicated and awe-inspiring contraption, which, when attached to headphones (thirty shillings) and acoustically tuned in with a tender scratching of the cat's whisker on the crystal, gave us a fugitive and intermittent programme from the BBC, London. A wireless set with valves (whatever they actually were) was as yet beyond our means.

But not beyond Florrie Forde's. She rested on one elbow and with the other hand twiddled the knobs on her glamorous wireless set; meanwhile she sang a slow song called 'Dream, Daddy'.

Auntie Gertie and I were home before my parents returned from the races. By the time they arrived the kitchen table was set for our tea. We hadn't yet sat down; my parents were full of which horses had won a place and which, in my father's words, were 'still coming up the field'. And what had we done with our day?

'We went to see Florrie Forde,' said Auntie Gertie, to such great amusement of my parents that my auntie looked at me in an almost fellow-juvenile amazement. My father and mother couldn't stop laughing. 'Gertie took her to see Florrie Forde,' my mother managed to splutter.

'They're killing themselves laughing,' murmured my auntie.

And why they were standing there laughing in the kitchen, falling into each other's arms in their mirth, I did not know and will never know.

Mrs Rule, Fish Jean and The Kaiser

I was fascinated from the earliest age I can remember by how people arranged themselves. I can't remember a time when I was not a person-watcher, a behaviourist. I was also an avid listener. It seems to me that my parents' friends and the people who called at our small flat were endless. I can remember the names and faces of people dating from my pre-school years far better than any others at any other period of my life.

Most important to me were Mrs Rule and her husband Professor Rule. They were a young American couple; he, originally from New Zealand, was already a Presbyterian minister but was doing a further course in theology at the University of Edinburgh. They stayed with us for a time, during which a pretty baby (born in a nursing home in Edinburgh) appeared. I looked over the crib at this wonder. I also recall how impressed my mother was when Professor Rule washed the baby's clothes. I remember Mrs Rule by the fireside with her dimples and an exciting set of cards one-inch square, each with a letter on it. With these she taught me to read, egged on by Andrew K. Rule DD, as I found out her husband was, when I was well able to read his name on an envelope. I was between the ages of three and four. It was an early start, although in Edinburgh at that time it was not unusual for children to read and write fluently before they were five. The firelight played on Mrs Rule's hands and face, on Professor Rule's bearded smile, and on my lettered, red-backed cards on a tray before me, as I sat at the fire on a low puffy stool, while Mrs Rule declared that a 't' and an 'h' together sounded 'th'. The Rules went home to America, from where they wrote letters to my mother, leaving with me the precious cards.

It is only more recently that I have been able to confirm the reality of my impressions of this exciting and kind couple. My brother tells me that Charlotte Rule played the piano excellently, which must have delighted my mother. Philip also remembers how beautiful she was. Charlotte Rule died after their return to the United States. The daughter of Andrew K. Rule's second marriage, Barbara Below, has been a valuable source of corroboration of the images of my infancy. When I told her, for instance, that her father taught us to make popcorn (and I can still see the popping corn in the pan held over the fire), Mrs Below confirmed that her father told her how, all those years ago, he showed his Scottish friends how to make popcorn.

I knew about everyone who wrote letters to my parents and everyone who called at the house. We had a spatially small life, and my mother could never forbear to comment on any happening. I used to love the doorbell to ring.

It was a joy to go out visiting with my mother. No special

26

arrangements were made to entertain children. We were just brought along, and we were expected to sit quietly. Not all children liked to do this, but for me it was better that way. I liked to listen. Not only did I feel at home with the immense list of characters who peopled our lives, and who largely ignored me, but there were also those whom I knew by hearsay, and often I touched people who had touched real history.

Such a person was Mrs Lipetz as she was to us, Susan to her husband. I was aware that she was elderly. She sat every afternoon at her bow-fronted window on their ground-floor flat in Bruntsfield Crescent, a sweep of tall houses that had been constructed in 1870 and that one could see from our front windows. Mrs Lipetz had been born in Alsace-Lorraine but spoke without a foreign accent. One day, when we went to see her, I heard her tell how, when she was a schoolgirl in Alsace-Lorraine, after the Franco-Prussian war, the children had to run and hide their French books because the Kaiser was visiting the school. This must have been in 1871, after the peace treaty of Frankfurt, when France ceded Alsace-Lorraine to the Germany of Kaiser Wilhelm I. And it still amazes me to reflect that the childhood experience of my friend Mrs Lipetz going back to 1871 coincided with the year of publication of *Middlemarch* by George Eliot, *The Descent of Man* by Charles Darwin and *Through the Looking Glass* by Lewis Carroll. At the time, of course, I had no historical awe, only an attraction to Mrs Lipetz's words 'run and hide our French books' and 'the Kaiser'. For a while I confused this Kaiser with the other Kaiser, his grandson, about whom people still talked. The Great War had only been over a few years. But then I was told that Mrs Lipetz's Kaiser was dead.

Another legendary character whom I missed by being born just too late was Fish Jean, who was much reminisced over by my father and his friends. ('Do you mind Fish Jean?' they would say, meaning, do you remember her?) Whether Fish Jean was the same as a certain Herrin' Jenny of Edinburgh fame, I doubt. It seems to me they were two characters, Herrin' Jenny probably fictional, preceding Fish Jean. The wonder of Fish Jean was not that, like other fish-wives of the fairly prosperous Newhaven fishing community, she went through the streets crying her wares, but that she did so in such flamboyant style. The driving seat of her horse-cart had to be made specially wide to take Fish Jean's great girth; she wore large diamond rings on all her fingers down to the knuckles, and would plunge these diamond-covered hands in amongst her glittering herrings and mackerels, proudly to serve her customers.

Another person I never met except through hearsay was Emmeline Pankhurst, the leader of the women's rights movement of those days. Their main aim was to obtain the vote for women. My maternal grandmother, Adelaide Uezzell, in the Watford group of the Suffragette movement (as they called themselves), had marched with Mrs Pankhurst, carrying an umbrella, as they all did. My grandmother told me about these events, from an early age. But it was too late for me to know or see Mrs Pankhurst. I had to imagine the scene.

Dead, both dead, Mrs Lipetz's Kaiser and my father's Fish Jean, before I could even set eyes on them. And my grandmother's Mrs Pankhurst – to me only an item of hearsay. This was something inexplicable.

Commodities

Shopping with my mother was a geography lesson, although she wouldn't have known it. There were grocers' shops with their sacks of beans and other products, and price tags stuck into them. Everything in those days came from somewhere. Rice came from Patna. Tea came from the then Ceylon. Bacon came from Ayrshire or Wiltshire. Beef came from Angus (it was marked Angus Beef).

Lamb and mutton came from Wales or Scotland when it didn't come from New Zealand.

Sometimes butter, too, came from New Zealand, but mainly from nearby Dumfries.

Cream came from Ayrshire, Cornwall or Devon.

Cheese came from Cheddar. I remember no other in my pre-school days. Later we had Gorgonzola all the way from Gorgonzola.

Fish came from the North Sea or (for the best herring) Loch Fyne. Besides herrings there were mackerel, John Dory, haddock, halibut, turbot, plaice, flounders and sole.

'Caller herrin" meant fresh herring. The popular ballad went:

> Wha'll buy my caller herrin'?
> They're bonny fish and halesome farin'.
> Wha'll buy my caller herrin'?
> New drawn frae the Forth.

Cotton came from India or Egypt. Silk came from Milan and Lyons. Lisle thread (for our stockings and summer underwear) came from Lille (formerly Lisle) in France.

Straw hats came from Leghorn or Panama.

Money was pounds (paper notes) or, equally, sovereigns (gold), silver half-crowns (eight to the pound), silver florins (ten to the pound), silver shillings (twenty made one pound), sixpenny bits (silver, half a shilling), tiny silver threepenny bits (half a sixpence), bronze pennies (known as 'coppers', twelve to one shilling), and, of the same alloy, halfpennies (pronounced 'haypnies', half a penny), and farthings (half a halfpenny). There were also genteel guineas, but there were no notes or coins for these. A guinea merely meant one pound plus one shilling. Doctors sent in their bills in guineas, as did furriers and high-class dressmakers and hatters. The best clothes shops marked their wares in guineas, but children's clothes were in pounds, shillings and pence, as were food and railway tickets.

My mother and father were obviously unaware of the custom that furriers were paid in guineas. I remember a local furrier, Mrs Madge Forrester, a large-bosomed lady, had been altering a fur cape of my mother's for a prequoted price that my parents took to be five pounds but which the furrier insisted was guineas. Mrs Forrester sat in the bow window of our sitting-room, having delivered the restructured fur cape; she was silhouetted against the light, repeating, 'No, not five pounds, five guineas. I said *five*. We furriers always mean guineas. I said *five*.' I remember my father forking out the extra five shillings in question; and always afterwards my parents referred to Mrs Forrester as 'I said Five'. They loved to repeat the phrase after each other. 'I said Five' lived and worked opposite our house, so we saw her frequently from the window. 'Good afternoon, Mrs Forrester,' my mother would say, passing her in the street. But later she would tell my father, 'I saw "I said Five".'

Neighbours

Meeting people in the street meant that you stopped and talked or you said something about the weather and went on. If the weather was good the amiable comment was 'Good morning, Mrs X. Fine day.' If it was raining, blowing hard from the north or snowing, the words in passing were 'Good morning, Mrs X. Seasonable weather.' First names were never used. Amongst the older Edinburgh women it was not unusual to address a married lady as Mistress X instead of Mrs. All during the 'thirties a very elderly and well-educated friend, Mrs Hardie, called my mother 'Mistress Camberg'.

On the ground floor of the block of flats next to ours was a jeweller's shop, the back premises of which were occupied by the owners, the Page family. On Sunday mornings Mr Page used to go to the Mound, which is the panoramic Hyde Park Corner of

Edinburgh, there to set up his box and preach the Bible, or about the Bible. What his message was I do not know. At the Mound on Sundays everyone and anyone was, and still is, permitted to say their say about anything, mainly politics or religion, so long as it isn't obscene or seditious in a fairly large sense. On Sunday afternoons, his duty fulfilled, red-haired Mr Page would set off with his motorbike and side-car to the country. His red-haired son James, still a schoolboy, rode on the pillion while Mrs Page sat in the side-car with their small daughter, Isabel, on her knee. My brother and I were both red-heads and so I considered it right that there should be some red-haired neighbours. The percentage of red-heads in Scotland is always comparatively high.

Isabel was exactly my age, and my first playmate. The back windows of our flats looked out on a pretty stretch of greens which formed a large grassy courtyard within four sides of a street block. And there we could play safely under the watchful glances of our mothers from their respective windows. Isabel and I played with our dolls, pitched a rudimentary tent or embarked on digging a hole to Australia until it was time to be called in to tea. Scottish summer days are long. The weather cannot always have been good enough for us to play outside, but when we did the sunlight went on for ever. On miraculous days Mrs Kerr, our upstairs neighbour, would open her window at about three in the afternoon and let down a picnic in a basket. I don't remember what exactly this picnic consisted of, except that we were always delighted with it and ate it all up.

Mrs Kerr was a good deal older than my mother. Her daughter, Maudie, was already in her twenties, training to be a singer. She had a job in the Civil Service, but a career as a singer was her ambition, testified to night after night from the flat above. We never complained, even amongst ourselves. It was accepted that Maudie was in a destined category. Mrs Kerr told us about Maudie's training in legendary tones meant to impress us as much as they actually did. Maudie was to sing in a concert:

'Of course she has to eat liver for her voice.' Great bouquets of flowers were ordered to be made up, so that they should be handed to blonde, blue-eyed Maudie on the stage. 'They all do it,' said Mrs Kerr. 'All singers get their own bouquets sent up to them on the stage.'

It was Mrs Kerr who taught my mother to make soup. 'Three brees to a bane,' said Mrs Kerr, which sounded shivery and poetic to me, like a line from a Border ballad. But I quickly realized what she meant: you got three brews out of every bone.

I seldom had difficulty understanding what people meant. Later, when I went to school, the kindly policeman who took me across the road didn't ask me what I was called, he said, 'What do they cry you?' We never used this idiom ourselves but many people around us cried a spade a spade. Our next-door neighbour, poor bedridden Miss Peggy Moffat, who was arthritic and had once been a painter, spoke plain English with a Scottish accent, but her housekeeper, Miss Draper, a wiry and scornful sooth-sayer, spoke much of the dialect; so that, when I won a prize at school, Miss Draper's disconcerting comment was 'The Deil aye kens his ain' which I well knew to mean 'The Devil always knows his own.' I would have been horrified if Miss Moffat herself had said anything like this, but as it was only Miss Draper being her true self, I bore no resentment at all. One of Peggy Moffat's oil paintings, of a glade in the botanical gardens, adorned our walls. That she would never wield a brush again had been her destiny before I was born. I liked to go to visit her and stand by her high bed which I could just see over the side of.

Downstairs, next door on the right, was Miss Morrison's sweet shop, where she stood with tall authority, her side of the counter having been built up higher than the customer's side. If you went there without your mother to buy a pennyworth of chocolate drops, of liquorice all-sorts, or a ha'pennyworth of hundreds-and-thousands, or a swirling barley-stick, Miss Morrison would enquire closely as to where you got that penny or that ha'penny, who gave it to you; and she would further interrogate you as to whether your mother knew you were spending those coins, held between your fingers, on sweeties. Only after satisfying herself on these and other deeply moral points would she take down the sweetie jar and weigh out the just portion; and even then she cautioned us to go straight home with our purchase and not eat it all up out there in the street. It was generally considered ill-mannered for parents to give money to young children to spend willy-nilly.

Some doors to the left was a large shoeshop, Lauders', now a Chinese restaurant. We never bought our shoes at Lauders', but I remember a pale daughter, a girl of about fifteen, very thin, green and grey, who stood by the window looking out. William Todd, the grocer, was at the end of the block, as it turns into Viewforth. He was important, because he had a licence to sell wines. Gilbey's port, four shillings and sixpence a bottle, was the great favourite with my mother; she sipped it throughout the day: 'my tonic'. Mr Todd gave a penny back on each empty bottle. And round the corner from Todd's was the home of the two ladies to whom my brother and I were sent to learn to play the piano, for although my mother had been a music teacher she didn't feel equal to teaching her own children. Among all the names of my infancy, those two sisters' names are among the very few that escape me. I know their house had a funny smell and that one of them had her stocking always twisted. My brother attended assiduously to his piano lesson. I much preferred to play with the parrot, which fascinated me, both at the time and later, in my thoughts. At first my hand could not yet quite stretch an octave. I did a five-finger exercise. Eventually my brother and I learned to play a tinkling duet, to my mother's pride.

In the next block, in Bruntsfield Place, was William Christie's butcher shop where gruesome carcasses of animals hung on hooks, the floor covered with sawdust, and jellied meats were displayed in the window under fearful names like 'potted head'. But Bill Christie was a sweet man, who became an important

33

part of my mother's life many many years later.

The main feature of interest in the large draper's shop on the opposite side of the street was a system of overhead pneumatic tubes that carried containers of money from the customer, via the assistant, to the counting house, and sent back the change. The shop assistant wrapped our money in the invoice and packed it into an egg-shaped receptacle that she pulled down from a wire dangling above her head. This would then shoot up and away. On its return a bell would ring and the assistant would reach up and pull down our change wrapped in its cocoon. I used to love to watch these money-containers whizzing between the various departments and the glassed-in office.

Next door to this draper's shop was glamorous Rudloff the hairdresser, with a model bust of a beautiful, blushing lady in the window, her short hair waved incredibly.

Just round the corner in Viewforth lived Nita McEwen, who resembled me very much. She was already in her first year at James Gillespie's School when I saw her with her parents, walking between them, holding their hands. I was doing the same thing. I was not yet at school. It must have been a Saturday or Sunday, when children used to walk with their parents. My mother remarked how like me the little girl was; one of her parents must have said the same to her. I looked round at the child and saw she was looking round at me. Either her likeness to me or something else made me feel strange. I didn't yet know she was called Nita. Later, at school, although Nita was in a higher class and we never played together, our physical resemblance was often remarked upon. Her hair was slightly redder than mine. Years later, when I was twenty-one, I was to meet Nita McEwen in a boarding house in the then Southern Rhodesia, now Zimbabwe. There, our likeness to each other was greatly remarked on. One night, Nita was shot dead by her husband, who then shot himself. I heard two girl's screams followed by a shot, then another shot. That was the factual origin of my short story 'Bang-Bang You're Dead'.

Myths and Images

I must have been very young when I made furrowed fields and ditches out of my dinner, with a fork, before eating it, but I well remember doing so. I used to like to have green spinach, yellow turnips, mashed potatoes and brown minced meat on my plate to produce the full pictorial effect. The fork made the ploughed furrows, and spaces between the food made ponds and rivers. It made eating more interesting, it added another dimension, as in *nouvelle cuisine*.

Sometimes I would be out with my parents when darkness fell, probably on a Saturday, when my father didn't go to work. In winter it was dark between three and four in the afternoon. We came home by tram-car from whose windows I could see the lights of the city making patterns in the distance. If we were walking I might get tired, and my father would carry me the last part of the way home; then, the lights of the city bobbed up and down against the dark blue sky.

Electricity had come to the principal streets of Edinburgh long before I was born, but in our Bruntsfield Place the street lamps were still lit by gas. We had progressed from the days of Robert Louis Stevenson's lamp-lighter ('With lantern and with ladder he comes posting up the street'); our gas-lamps had pilot lights, so that the lamp-lighter who passed by at dusk came posting with a long pole in his hand, with which he deftly turned on the lamp-light. Like Stevenson, I used to wait at the window to witness this performance, and a few years later, when I came to possess *A Child's Garden of Verses*, I felt a close affinity with our long-dead Edinburgh writer, on the basis of more than one shared experience. The Braid Hills, the Blackford Hill and Pond, the Pentland Hills of Stevenson's poems, his 'hills of home' were mine, too.

My pre-school dresses were not made of stuff like other children's. They were knitted in silk and wool by my mother and Auntie Gertie in a variety of colours, among which I remember

35

royal blue, bronze, and old gold. My simple white silk knitted dress for parties had a feather stitch. Many small girls at parties had ballerina-type dresses. The small boys generally wore kilts. We all carried our party shoes in a special bag and changed into them inside the house, something that I do to this day. To make my house shoes more partified my mother would mould a rosette of pink sealing-wax on the front of each one. Parties were for Christmas or birthdays. Christmas was largely a children's feast in the Scotland of those days. Many shops, offices and factories remained open on Christmas Day; the great day was New Year's. Friends would come first-footing shortly after midnight on Hogmanay (New Year); for luck, a dark man was preferable.

At Hallowe'en (31 October) children with blackened faces and grotesque clothes used to come round the doors collecting pennies: 'Please to help the guisars' (guisards or mummers).

But at Christmas, already the English custom of hanging up our stockings had arrived, and I duly hung up mine. My brother Philip, more ambitious, hung up a pillow case. My brother, who was clever with his hands, often made cut-out toys for me which wouldn't fit into my stocking, and were spread all around it at the foot of my bed.

The dispenser of presents at parties was called Santie, and was dressed in his traditional uniform. Santie usually spoke with a broad accent, he cried us bairns, like the policeman. I remember only once getting a present out of Santie's sack that I wasn't thrilled with. This was a religious, positively Calvinistic, picture book about Baby Jesus and the dire consequences to children who didn't fit the required standards. My mother, at home, pronounced my hostess a damn fool for giving such books to children, thus shaking any illusion I might still have had about the reality of Santie.

One party I remember was at the house of my school-friend of many years, Frances Niven. We were still quite tiny. I came to love this house, at Howard Place, adjoining the house where

Robert Louis Stevenson was born. At the party of my memory, the children, about twenty of us, were settled at a long table in the large, festively decorated pantry next to the kitchen. We were given some kind of orange mousse, served prettily in half-orange skins, and we ate this with teaspoons. Frances's mother and aunt, and some other elders, were hovering around. One of them said, 'Look at them tucking in!' I seemed to be the only child who heard this, and although I didn't make any fuss, I was ridiculously affected. I thought it a terrible thing to say, and I put down my spoon, unable to finish my delicious orange sweet. Perhaps I felt that no one would have made such an embarrassing remark at a grown-up party. Fortunately nobody noticed that I'd stopped eating.

My mother used to come and collect me when it was time to go home. Her black hair had been cut short by Rudloff and she wore powder and paint, as make-up was called. The powder was Coty's, shade Rachel. The paint was carmine, a red powder bought from the chemist in very small quantities, it nestled in the fold of a piece of white paper, and it cost tuppence (two pence). My mother was decidedly out of place amongst the northern worthies who came to collect my friends. My own hair must have been cut about that time, when many small girls had short hair, for I remember people saying to me, 'Where are your curls?'

What images return ... ! My father made rings with his cigarette smoke, he made the shadow of Queen Victoria in profile on the wall, and rabbits out of table-napkins. I learned to tell the time from his pocket watch.

'Coal!' would come the cry from the streets every morning, and when we needed coal the coalman's horse would bring his cart to a clicking stop at my mother's bidding from the window. Then up the stairs would tramp the coal-black man with his hundredweights to tip them into our coal cellar which was built into the flat. How heavy the word hundredweight sounded. Each sack cost half-a-crown. We used coal to heat the water and to

37

burn in the fireplaces. More than once, our chimney caught fire and my father had to go and pay a fine. Sometimes a chimney sweep, sootier even than the coalman, would come and clean the flues. This was done partly inside the house and partly on the roof. Two men were involved, calling up to each other an eerie 'ooh-whoo'.

'Rags, bottles or bones! Any old rags?' was another street cry that came wafting up to our windows. Why did he want to buy bones, I wondered, and still wonder. What bones, I thought. *Whose* bones? The rag-man had no horse. He pushed his cart by hand, and on it were piled old cartons, old pieces of furniture, kettles, tins.

My mother was full of superstitions and presentiments. She wouldn't wear green. But I knew that this was mad from the evidence of perfectly happy people I saw wearing green. Her terror of thunder and lightning likewise had no effect on me. She would huddle with me into a darkened room during a thunderstorm, but as soon as I got away on holiday to the seaside at Crail in Fife, I ran down to the wonderful beach to watch thunderstorms in progress over the North Sea.

For my mother, shoes on a table were bad luck. But who would put shoes on a table? Crossed cutlery was a bad omen. My mother turned over her money in her purse when she saw the new moon and bowed three times to it, no matter who was watching her. (I still do this, myself. True, I do it for fun; but all the same I do it.) She and her mother were fond of quoting maxims. My grandmother:

> A whistling woman, a crowing hen
> Is neither fit for God nor man.

My mother (rousing herself to action): 'This won't pay the old woman her ninepence;' 'Laugh before seven, cry before eleven;'

and (burdensome forewarning to me) 'A son's a son till he gets a wife, but a daughter's a daughter all her life.' There was also the oft-repeated, 'The eyes are the windows of the soul.' (She herself had lovely large brown eyes.)

My father's sayings were more humorous and savoured of the music-hall. If there was a lull in the conversation he might say, 'If this weather continues, we'll have no change.' And setting forth for a walk: 'Take my arm and call me Lucy.' There was also a mysterious person named by my father 'Mr Poomschtok', whose chief characteristic was that he didn't exist, so that a great many happenings could be attributed to him. My father also performed a strange dance to the tune of 'In a Persian Market'. He did another country-type dance, holding in his fingers the knees of his trousers as if they were a skirt.

When he took my mother to a dance, he wore an evening suit with a white scarf and kid gloves, which, I was told, he kept on while dancing, as was the custom. My mother went out in a white beaded dress with an uneven hem, which made her square in shape but was greatly approved of by Auntie Gertie.

On fine Sundays we would walk on the Braid Hills or round the Blackford Pond, and in the summer we would go with spades and pails and sandwiches on the tram-car to the sands at Portobello for the day.

I was woken in the middle of the night and taken to the window to see the fireworks in the back greens. 'It's 1922!' my mother said. I was given some warm port-wine.

I had measles and saw my face in the mirror, all red freckles. Dr Thatcher arrived in his black frock-coat, or morning coat, as it was sometimes called, his striped trousers, and his top hat which he placed upside down on the bed, while my mother stood aside, more concerned about the clean towel and basin of water for the doctor to wash his hands than she was about me. The tram-cars rattled past while Dr Thatcher bade me say 'Ah,' and frowned against their noise. Dr Thatcher knew about my mother's much-vaunted nervous breakdown, which she had had some years before I was born. She still boasted a nervous condition, in so far as she couldn't be left in the house quite alone; she was afraid. But she could go out alone. I took this robustly for granted; it was part of life.

Legends and stories of that time before I was born were also enfolded in the passing of the day. My father, the youngest of eleven, had run away to sea at the age of fourteen. He reached Kirkwall in the Orkneys, very seasick, and was put ashore at the local police station where his father came from Edinburgh to recover him. There was the story of his engagement to my mother long ago – it must have been 1909 – and of how the engagement was at one time broken off at the insistence of my mother's Aunt Sarah; this worthy woman learned that my father had given my mother a pair of gloves. It was regarded with blank horror for a man to present an unmarried girl with what was termed an item of apparel. It was the end of the world. I don't know how the affair was put right. But the end of the world, the Great War, did come to pass, and had passed, before I was four years old and heard this story, now a matter of amusement. Just about the time I was born society was changing rapidly.

I never knew my paternal grandparents, who were known to their family as 'Pa' and 'poor Ma'. It was said that poor Ma could sit on her hair and that she sat reading the Bible by the window all day. I imagined her doing both at the same time.

The Doorbell

That ring at the door that I loved so much would bring, in the afternoon, my mother's friends or, on rare occasions, my married aunts. In the evening a much more exciting variety of family friends rang the bell, many of them fairly eccentric, in whom I took a deep interest.

Only a few months ago I had a letter from one of my parents' friends, an American who was then a young medical student, Jay Snyder, who recalls that (at a date much later than my pre-school infancy) as a child I was very shy and used to run and hide under the table. I believe this must be true; a table covered by a long cloth is a good hiding place and listening post for children. Still, I can't for the life of me remember this. As an infant I was certainly shy, as were most children. We were all discouraged from showing off, and unless invited to recite a poem or play or sing, we wouldn't open our mouth.

A pulley on the landing, or doorlifter as we called it, would open the street door for visitors who pulled that wonderful doorbell. In those days before I went to school, people were far more important to me than toys or nature. The beauty of walks over the hills and by the sea was beginning to seep into my consciousness by way of the sensations of smell and of sheer liberty and the lyrical suggestiveness of nature-verse, but it had not yet formed a positive delight in my mind such as people presented.

The magic pulley on the landing would often admit a voice first of all, calling up the stairs, for there was a curve in the staircase and one could not see immediately who the visitor was. Then on stage to us, as it seemed, came one of the following:

Miss Pride, her small face covered with tiny red veins, in a neat brown coat and hat, fawn gloves, and fawn wool stockings. What she had to do with my parents, what was the basis of their friendship, I can't think. She was neither of the race of Auntie Gertie, who practised the Charleston with my mother on the kitchen waxcloth, nor was she of the class of tall, fair, gentle Fanny Pagan, then wife of a bus-driver, who used to come and give my mother a hand in scrubbing floors, and who later was widowed, and remarried well, and was widowed again, and, still beautiful, had a special friendship with my father; and who, what's more, after his death, was to become my mother's best friend. Sweet Fanny Pagan! Fanny was still mainly a character of the future, but even now she had nothing whatever to do with Miss Pride of the present. This I knew perfectly well, as Miss Pride sat primly chatting with a clipped voice, and drinking her cup of tea. I never knew Miss Pride's first name.

There was Miss Macdonald whose name was Margaret, as I gathered from a piece of conversation she reported. Miss Macdonald was dressed in navy blue with a white blouse. She was finer-bred than Miss Pride, but it was said she was not all there. I think my parents were sorry for her. All the time she spoke tears coursed down her cheek. They trickled down into her cup of tea. She couldn't ever stop crying. She was bound up in a court case against someone who had wrongly accused her. Her brother, a lawyer, couldn't do much more than he had already done. The word 'like' peppered her conversation. 'My brother, like, wouldn't go, like, any further with it, like ... '

Bella Myers, large-hipped and full of cheer, was much less of a puzzle, and a much closer friend. Nobody understood why she hadn't married except that she was less beautiful than her married sister, Gertie Rosenbloom. She brought stories of her office life, she discussed music, she gossiped wildly about people. She reported office puns, such as 'Many are cauld [Scottish for cold] but few are chosen,' the heating in her place of work having broken down. Bella Myers hardly noticed my presence; which, to me, was all to the good.

Another of the random and varied characters that the doorbell brought was a Bavarian fräulein whose name I can't remember. She was tubby and had a large round face with reddish-gold hair drawn back in a bun. I am not clear what she was doing in Edinburgh but I think she was a private nurse. How did my parents know her? Later in the 'thirties this lady disappeared; my mother supposed she had been 'called back' to Germany by Hitler. The same applied to a young philosopher, also reddish in colouring, who sometimes frequented our house. He went for walking tours. Mr Anchutz was his name. He had nothing to do with the Bavarian woman; their visits never coincided. He spent a great deal of time urging my parents to vote Labour. But, more understandably since he was a university man, he too went back. And I wonder, indeed, what happened to him.

Mary Wright was an afternoon crony of my mother's, flighty, powdered and painted and fox-furred. She was the mother of Billy who, with my brother, dressed me up as a boy and plastered back my hair with water, so that I caught a cold. The Patersons with their schoolgirl daughters Doris, especially dear to my mother, and Consie (Constance), were most glamorous of all. There was a son, Atholl, a grown schoolboy on whom I took a shine, and whom I would follow everywhere. I remember following him over stretch upon stretch of grass, and picking up windfall apples; I suppose this was in the Patersons' garden.

The Royal Visit

I learned that children could be born out of wedlock, and I gathered this information in a very simple way. The King (George V) and Queen Mary came on an official visit to Edinburgh. For this animated occasion our friend Mrs Hardie (or, as she preferred, Mistress Hardie), who was then an active ninety, had obtained seats on the balcony of a smart shop in Princes Street. I sat between Mrs Hardie and my mother. We were right in the front. Flags were flying everywhere, all up Princes Street. Mrs Hardie sat very erect as was her wont. It was a lovely sunny day. The royal entrance began: carriages, horses, plumes bobbing up and down. Kilts, bagpipes. The first carriage, flanked, in state, by cavalry, contained a gentleman with a cocked hat, uniform and a pointed beard. 'The police escort,' murmured my mother, 'Chief Constable Ross.' At this, Mrs Hardie leaned across me and touched my mother's arm. 'That's King Edward's bairn,' she said. As is common with adults, she didn't think for a moment that a child would understand her. I didn't quite understand at first, although I knew that King Edward had been the present King's father. Then came the enlightenment: the next carriage contained a gentleman almost the twin image of Chief Constable Ross. With his plumed hat, gleaming uniform and pointed beard, he would have been the Chief Constable all over again, except that, with pink-and-white Queen Mary, wearing her usual toque, at his side, and his arm raised in salutes and greetings, he was obviously King George V, another of King Edward's bairns. I put two and two together, full of wonder, while Mrs Hardie proceeded to explain to my mother that Queen Mary's beautiful complexion was 'all enamel'.

1923

My aunts and uncles, my cousins, were another world. My mother's family, the Uezzells, lived in Watford where we went for our summer holidays. My maternal grandmother and grandfather were there, in their shop of all sorts in the High Street. They lived above and at the back of the shop, but there was room for us all. It was always the first fortnight of September when we went to Watford on the puffing and clanging overnight train, changing at London. Somehow I gained and noted the information, irrelevant to me at the time, that this annual jaunt cost a total of eight pounds.

My Watford cousins were at this time five in number, but since I clearly remember six, I presume that my memory of the whole family only stretches back to a later time after I went to school, when the youngest, Alec, was born. Four were red-heads with my Auntie Alice and Phil Uezzell. They lived in a different part of Watford from my grandparents, who kept the shop in front of their house and chickens at the back.

My more vivid recollections of my Edinburgh aunts and cousins refer to a later time in my childhood. This is because they seldom rang the doorbell at random. We tended to pay and return visits to our relations when they were expected. When my aunts Rae and Esther did call unexpectedly it was always in the late afternoon, and they always put my mother in a flap. Rae was a fresh-air fiend and insisted on my mother throwing open all the windows, complaining that our house was stuffy. Auntie Rae was a Francophile; the best compliment she could pay was 'very *French*'. Esther, the eldest of my father's family, was a practising, if not absolutely orthodox, Jew and my mother was always anxious to hide from Esther evidence of ham, bacon, pork sausages or any other unholy delicacy that she had in mind to prepare for our high tea, when my father and Gertie should come home from their work. But Auntie Esther took a keen interest in my reading and writing, and I loved her for that. I remember her best at a time when I was wearing my dark red (we called it maroon) school blazer and could show her my first school-books.

In the summer of 1923 I already had my new school-books, ready to start school in September. Nelson's Infant Primer, bought at Baxendine's in Chambers Street, was my first reading book. I read it avidly all summer and still have a detailed impression of the pastoral illustrations (for nobody, in those story-books, lived in a city). My brother, now on his school holidays, was making a model of the Forth Bridge with his Meccano set; it was augmented by various spare parts that my father brought home from his work place, having made them specially with his own hands. Those summer evenings of Edinburgh go on till ten at night, and I would see from the window the golfers returning with their cleeks (as we called golf clubs) in their hands from their round of golf on the Bruntsfield Links where my school-to-be was situated. My brother also played golf; I was promised a putter for next year. My mother lingered at the piano on the long summer evenings. I had a pencil case and some new-smelling notebooks to go with my Infant Primer. I had outdoor shoes with laces to tie up as well as my normal house shoes with a strap to button up with a button hook. I had a black velour hat with a red and yellow band and a JGS monogrammed badge on it. The yellow JGS stood for James Gillespie's School. On my maroon blazer pocket was another badge, a rampant yellow unicorn surmounting the school motto: *Fidelis et Fortis*. My parents had informed themselves that this meant Faithful and Strong. How clever we all were!

I don't know at what point before I went to school I became aware of poor men or women, sometimes accompanied by children, singing for pennies in the back green. When my mother told me they were hungry, I looked out at them with tears. Usually my mother wrapped up a penny in a piece of newspaper and threw it out, as did a few others among our neighbours. No one remarked on the quality of the performance, the singing itself; it would have seemed irrelevant. This was part of the distress following the First World War. The men who had returned could not find work and the social services were inadequate. I once saw a child of about seven selling newspapers at Tollcross on a winter night, without so much as a vest underneath the thin jacket of his coat. He was barefoot. My mother was dismayed. Such children were mostly destined to die of tuberculosis. It was said, I think truly, that their parents drank every penny they could lay hands on, including their children's gains. Children clustered outside the smelly public houses as we passed, waiting for their elders. I was not exposed to many of these sights but certainly before I went to school I was conscious that others suffered. Poor as we certainly were, there were others greatly poorer, positively in want, and I, in the safety of holding my parents' hands, saw it.

Sometimes I compare my early infancy with that of my friends whose very early lives were in the hands of nannies, and who were surrounded by servants and privilege. Those pre-school lives seem nothing like so abundant as mine was, nothing like so crammed with people and with amazing information. I was not set aside from adult social life, nor cosied-up in a nursery, and taken for nice regular walks far from the madding crowd. I was witness to the whole passing scene. Perhaps no other life could ever be as rich as that first life, when, five years old, prepared and briefed to my full capacity, I was ready for school.

CHAPTER TWO

From the sixteenth century to the nineteenth, the worthy and prosperous merchants and burghers of Edinburgh vied with each other to leave their fortunes for the founding of schools throughout the city. Education was held in awe, and the Scottish idea was that nobody should be denied this privilege. The schools, only a few of them having undergone change in nature and in buildings, still exist.

Heriot's School, founded by George Heriot, otherwise known as Jingling Geordie, still flourishes. Jingling Geordie was a jeweller, goldsmith and moneylender to James VI of Scotland (I of England). Daniel Stewart, an exchequer officer, endowed a school that still stands in its turreted splendour of 1814. Mary Erskine, 'relict of James Hair, druggist', left a fortune for the foundation, in 1707, of the girls' school named after her. Fettes College was founded by Sir William Fettes, a late eighteenth-century tea and wine merchant and Lord Provost of Edinburgh. George Watson, an early eighteenth-century merchant and first accountant at the Bank of Scotland, left considerable funds for the foundation of today's boys' schools and girls' schools which bear his name. James Donaldson, publisher of the late eighteenth and early nineteenth centuries, left a fortune that now provides a school for deaf children, Donaldson's Hospital. And splendid Andrew Carnegie, whom we all know by his bequests to universities and libraries, came from a linen-weaver's family in

Dunfermline, close to Edinburgh. Carnegie's endowments included handsome trusts for a school and library in Dunfermline, and for Scottish universities, among them the University of Edinburgh, of which he was Rector.

When James Gillespie, a snuff merchant, died, in 1797, a part of his fortune went to found a day school for boys and girls. This was the school that it fell to my happy lot to attend. Gillespie's endowment allowed for parents like my own, of high aspirations and slender means, to pay moderate fees in return for educational services far beyond what they were paying for. When I first attended, at the age of five, it was coeducational but after some years we lost our little boys and we were James Gillespie's High School for Girls, to this day one of Edinburgh's best-known schools.

I spent twelve years at Gillespie's, the most formative years of my life, and in many ways the most fortunate for a future writer.

The infant department led to the very top, grade by grade. Never were we allowed to forget the history of our dear Mr Gillespie, a frugal but benevolent bachelor. Each year on Founder's Day the school gathered for a ceremony which began, on the earliest occasion I remember, with the 'Our Father' and ended in general hilarity as the pupils watched the staff, on the platform, take a pinch of snuff in honour of the Founder's profession. Founder's Day was held on a Friday in June. While our elders recovered from their sneezes the senior prefect always put up an eloquent and prolonged plea on behalf of a holiday for the school on the following Monday, which was invariably granted. In between these opening and closing events would come a homily, reminding us of the worthy Gillespie legends. In the 1930s, the snuff-taking ceremony was waived.

The story of James Gillespie, Esq. of Spylaw, is in many ways the most charming of all the merchants' histories, he was so satisfactorily and completely an Edinburgh character. He was humbly born, a son of the people. He is depicted with a shrewd eye; his bulbous nose and protuberant chin form a nutcracker profile; his mouth has the set of prosperity.

James Gillespie and his elder brother John went into the snuff and tobacco business in the early part of the eighteenth century. James had his own mill in the Edinburgh district of Spylaw while his brother ran a tobacconist shop in the High Street. Neither brother married. They had a reputation for extreme frugality and at the same time, benevolence. The Gillespies flourished all the more when the American War caused a scarcity of tobacco and sent up the price. I like to reflect on the fact that my good schooling is partly due to the American War of Independence. James appears to have outlived his brother, working on to a ripe age and accumulating a large fortune. He kept a carriage, and the story is told that, meeting a friend of the nobility, James asked him to suggest a motto to place upon it. The friend (Henry Erskine) obliged with the couplet:

> Wha wad hae thocht it
> That noses had bocht it.

Gillespie put nothing of the kind on his carriage, content with only his initials. A memoir of this fine old man records:

Mr Gillespie lived among his workmen in homely and patriarchal style, and though far from being miserly was extremely frugal and industrious, his favourite maxim being 'Waste not, want not.' Even in extreme age one might have seen him with an old blanket round him and a night-cap on, both covered with snuff, attending the mill and superintending the operations of his man, Andrew Fraser.

There was one young man, evidently a relation, whom James Gillespie brought up as his heir; but Gillespie's death revealed that this, his next of kin, was disinherited. It sounds a mean act on the part of the Laird of Spylaw, reputed as he was to have sat at the table familiarly with his servants, to have been an exceptionally indulgent landlord, to have nourished affection for his horse and cared greatly for his household animals and livestock. Why did James Gillespie disinherit the younger man? It is said that he did not want to indulge in the vanity of being remembered by a thing called after himself. There is no verification for the story beyond a history of the Parish of Colinton written while James Gillespie's name was 'still green' in the parish. It was certainly an attitude typical of Edinburgh to deny feelings for the sake of principle, and maybe that is the chilly truth about the disinheritance of the young Gillespie. Certainly, no member of his family benefited at all from James Gillespie's will.

His fortune was originally left in trust for a hospital and a school for poor boys. Gradually the object of the charity was changed until a modest fee-paying establishment, James Gillespie's School for boys and girls, came under the benefit of his foundation. For most of my school-days it fell under the care of the Edinburgh Education Authority, and after 1929, was mainly for girls. Today, it is a state board school, coeducational. What happened to James Gillespie's money is a question that has cropped up throughout all these changes, never failing to occupy correspondence columns in the newspapers. Some say that the funds were simply absorbed by the Edinburgh educational authorities. An interesting point is that at a committee meeting in 1938 the school was reported to be overcrowded with a membership of fourteen hundred girls. There was a waiting list of four hundred. As a solution to the problem it was proposed to raise the fees. To which the chairman replied, 'Every time we have increased the fees the number of pupils desiring to attend has risen.'

Despite the introduction of fee-paying, one of the main benefits to be derived from James Gillespie's fortune was the system of bursaries and scholarships which enabled the more intelligent girls from free schools to attend Gillespie's, while girls already at Gillespie's who obtained sufficiently good marks could continue their higher education without further fees. This was a godsend to parents like mine, who could not afford the rising cost of education. After the age of twelve I did not involve my parents in school fees.

The official religion of James Gillespie's School was Presbyterian of the Church of Scotland; much later this rule was expanded to include Episcopalian doctrines. But in my day Tolerance was decidedly the prevailing religion, always with a puritanical slant. Nothing can be more puritanical in application than the virtues. To enquire into the differences between the professed religions around us might have been construed as Intolerance.

Many religious persuasions were represented among the pupils. There were Jewish girls in practically every class. I remember one Hindu Indian named Coti whom we made much of. There were lots of Catholics. Some girls were of mixed faiths – mother Protestant, father Jewish; Irish Catholic mother, Episcopalian father. It meant very little in practical terms to us. The Bible appeared to cover all these faiths, for I don't remember any segregation during our religious teaching, although in other classes some pupils may have sat apart, simply 'listening in'.

Scotland was historically rich in sects. James Gillespie himself was an admirer of the Covenanters, those worthy bearers of Bible and sword who rebelled against the imposition of the English liturgy on the Scots in the seventeenth century. The Covenanters could be said to be reformers of the Reformation. But James Gillespie went further than that. He inclined towards a stricter sect, the Cameronians, a section of the Scottish Covenanters named after their chief exponent, Richard Cameron. In 1743, during James Gillespie's lifetime, they became the Reformed Presbyterians. Politically, they strongly opposed the union of England and Scotland.

One Founder's Day, Friday 12 June 1931, after the ceremony,

twenty-five Gillespie girls set off for the Covenanters' Grave in the Pentland Hills to sing the Scottish paraphrase of the One hundred and twenty-first Psalm in Mr James Gillespie's honour.

I to the hills will lift mine eyes
From whence doth come mine aid.
My safety cometh from the Lord
Who heaven and earth hath made.

The schoolhouse had been built in 1904, first for another school, Boroughmuir. But Gillespie's took over in 1914. It was an Edwardian type of building, and, for those days, modern inside, with large classrooms and big windows that looked out over the leafy trees, the skies and swooping gulls of Bruntsfield Links. From where I lived the school was a ten-minute walk through avenues of tall trees. Leading further away from the school was another avenue of hawthorns, flowering dark pink in May. We called these may-blossoms. The school was surrounded by the large public moorland of the Links. A very attractive cottage which had belonged to a fashionable photographer, 'Swan Watson's', was attached to the school, but shortly after my arrival, to our mixed sorrow and delight, it was pulled down to make way for an extension that comprised a wonderful science room, a spacious gymnasium and a totally new infants' department.

Of the infant school I remember comparatively little. My home life was still of the first importance, and remains imprinted in memories that I can still share with my brother Philip.

But of those first years at school I retain an impression of Plasticine-modelling, carol-singing and reading aloud (which I did well). A medal was circulated every week. One week I won it for a crayon drawing of a tomato. I remember my big red tomato on the dark brown drawing-paper background; I couldn't see anything very special about it. I played the triangle in the percussion band. All I had to do was bang it rhythmically, something that would have driven my parents mad at home. I played a milkmaid in a tableau.

There were always flowers in the classrooms, on the window sills and on the teachers' tables, all throughout my school-days. The girls or their parents usually provided these, but the teachers were always tending plants. Some of them would lift the flower-vases each morning to see if the cleaners had cleaned properly underneath. We had hyacinths in the spring. My mother sometimes put a bunch of daffodils in my hands to take to school in the afternoon.

The furnaces for the central heating were stoked by Jannie (the janitor, an ex-policeman whose real name was John Bremner). Jannie it was who, with his ally, Parkie (the park-keeper), kept an eye on the leafy meadows surrounding the school so that no potential molesters or peeping men in mackintoshes ever got near us. All the same, we were cautioned not to turn somersaults on the low iron railings that lined the pathways, lest 'passing men might see your underwear'. Alas, those iron railings went, like so much other civic ironwork, to make armaments in wartime, never to be replaced.

From the earliest days we each tended to have a special friend, our 'chum'. My chum until I was nine years old was Daphne Porter, an only child whose father had died 'out in India'. Daphne had been told about sex and she gave me her elementary version of the affair in a matter-of-fact way: I well remember that she was concentrating on something else, like making a daisy-chain, while she informed me what 'the gentleman' did to 'the lady'. We used to have tea at each other's houses after school. One day Daphne was absent, and many days went on into months. Daphne was in hospital and eventually died, taking all her information with her, and her very pretty looks. I had no idea what she died of. Her mother appeared like a ghostly wraith, walking along the street in deep mourning, which in the Edinburgh of those days consisted of a long black head-veil over a black coat, and black stockings and shoes. At the passing-by of Mrs Porter, I thought of the possibility of my own early death, and was far more unhappy for my mother's imagined grief than I was for myself. I didn't know what to say to Mrs Porter. I just walked along with her for a block. I don't think she knew what to say to me.

So for a while I had no chum, but soon I found another best friend, Frances Niven. I already knew Frances quite well. We were both deeply interested in poetry and imaginative writing of all kinds. From then, Frances was my closest friend all through my school-days.

The walls of our classrooms had hitherto been covered with our own paintings and drawings, records of travels, pages from the *National Geographic*, portraits of exotic animals and birds. But now I come to Miss Christina Kay, that character in search of an author, whose classroom walls were adorned with reproductions of early and Renaissance paintings, Leonardo da Vinci, Giotto, Fra Lippo Lippi, Botticelli. She borrowed these from the senior art department, run by handsome Arthur Couling. We had the Dutch masters and Corot. Also displayed was a newspaper cutting of Mussolini's Fascisti marching along the streets of Rome.

I fell into Miss Kay's hands at the age of eleven. It might well be said that she fell into my hands. Little did she know, little did I know, that she bore within her the seeds of the future Miss Jean Brodie, the main character in my novel, in a play on the West End of London and on Broadway, in a film and a television series.

I do not know exactly why I chose the name Miss Brodie. But recently I learned that Charlotte Rule, that young American woman who taught me to read when I was three, had been a Miss Brodie and a schoolteacher before her marriage. Could I have heard this fact and recorded it unconsciously?

In a sense Miss Kay was nothing like Miss Brodie. In another sense she was far above and beyond her Brodie counterpart. If she could have met 'Miss Brodie' Miss Kay would have put the fictional character firmly in her place. And yet no pupil of Miss Kay's has failed to recognize her, with joy and great nostalgia, in the shape of Miss Jean Brodie in her prime.

She entered my imagination immediately. I started to write about her even then. Her accounts of her travels were gripping, fantastic. Besides turning in my usual essays about how I spent my holidays I wrote poems about how she had spent her various holidays (in Rome, for example, or Egypt, or Switzerland). I thought her experiences more interesting than mine, and she loved it. Frances, too, fell entirely under her spell. In fact, we all did, as is testified by the numerous letters I have received from time to time from Miss Kay's former pupils.

I had always enjoyed watching teachers. We had a large class of about forty girls. A full classroom that size, with a sole performer on stage before an audience sitting in rows looking and listening, is essentially theatre.

From my first days at school I had been far more interested in the looks, the clothes, the gestures, of the individual teachers than I was in their lessons. With Miss Kay, I was fascinated by both. She was the ideal dramatic instructor, and it is not surprising that her reincarnation, Miss Brodie, has always been known as a 'good vehicle for an actress'.

It was not that Miss Kay overacted; indeed, she never acted at all. She was a devout Christian, deeply versed in the Bible. There could have been no question of a love-affair with the art master, or a sex-affair with the singing master, as in Miss Brodie's life. But children are quick to perceive possibilities, potentialities: in a remark, perhaps in some remote context; in a glance, a smile. No, Miss Kay was not literally Miss Brodie, but I think Miss Kay had it in her, unrealized, to be the character I invented.

Years and years later, some time after the publication of *The*

Prime of Miss Jean Brodie, Frances Niven (now Frances Cowell), my dear best friend of those days, observed in a letter:

> Surely 75% is Miss Kay? Dear Miss Kay! of the cropped iron grey hair with fringe (and heavy black moustache!) and undisputable admiration for Il Duce. Hers was the expression 'crème de la crème' – hers the revealing extra lessons on art and music that stay with me yet. She it was who took us both (who were especial favourites of hers –? – part of the as yet unborn Brodie Set) to see Pavlova's last performance at the Empire Theatre. Who took us for afternoon teas at McVities.

Frances and I were not alone in finding Miss Kay exhilarating and impressive. I don't think any one of us ever forgot her. One of her former pupils, Elizabeth Vance (formerly Betty Murphy), from a class following mine, has written to me about 'the wonderful years with Miss Kay'. Elizabeth was quick to recognize the element of our Miss Kay in Miss Brodie. A recent letter of hers from her home in Australia gives some flavour of Christina Kay's extra-curricular teaching. ('Teaching' is not quite the word, however. It was, rather, pure and riveting entertainment.) Here are part of Elizabeth's reminiscences:

> I wonder if Miss Kay had *one* Italian parent, or perhaps a grandparent, as I remember her with dark eyes and an olive complexion – and such a great love of Italy and its art treasures: the paintings, the statues, the buildings. I have never seen the Colosseum, the catacombs, the Sistine Chapel, the Ponte Vecchio or the Doges' Palace but through Miss Kay I feel I know them quite well. Interspersed with the Italian masters and the French Impressionists of the 19th century and the Dutch School (Rembrandt's portraits in particular) and literature and poetry and interior decorating (I moved all the ornaments on our sitting-room mantelpiece to form a more pleasing 'line') we still had such an excellent grounding

in the traditional three Rs (useful, even today). How *did* she manage it. With Miss Kay I *liked* mental arithmetic and long division and multiplication sums, and those spelling lists, and found grammar thoroughly enjoyable ...

But it is in another letter that Elizabeth Vance brings back to me the flavour and sense of Miss Kay in her classroom sixty years ago.

During recent scenes on television of the reunification of Germany, from Berlin, and over the sounds of bands playing and fireworks banging, I heard the commentator mention Unter den Linden – and I was back in Miss Kay's class and she was saying 'In Berlin there is a street called Unter den Linden – that means "under the lime trees", girls, and there are many furriers' shops in that street.'

'Many furriers' shops ... ' That was typical of those dazzling non-sequiturs of Miss Kay's which filled my young heart with joy. One could see in one's mind's eye a parade of rich overindulged German ladies, already swathed in furs, stepping out grandly under the lime trees of Berlin.

Cathie Davie (now Mrs Semeonoff), a brilliant scholar and school dux, was a senior girl when I was still a junior. She excelled at everything – acting, poetry-composition, mathematics, English. I had never known quite such an intellectual; even my clever cousin Mossie, who collected gold medals in medical school, seemed less intelligent. Cathie seemed unaware of her talents. I saw comparatively little of her but, as she lived near me and took the same route home at lunch-times and in the afternoons, I used to catch up with her and sometimes introduce a topic. Whatever it was she would discourse upon it without divergence while traversing the leafy avenues of the Links. I was fascinated. She discussed Chaucer or Spenser as living people, but living people she never discussed at all. Cathie was infinitely

59

kind. Of course, I was already known in the school as a poet. Some years ago, when someone had been making a claim in the newspapers for Miss Brodie's origin in a different teacher – the indefatigable and enthusiastic Alison Foster, of the upper school's English department – Cathie, who had experienced Miss Kay's classroom in her own junior years, was quick to inform the claimant that 'anyone who had been in her class knew that the character was based primarily on Miss Kay'.

When I first saw the film of *The Prime* my immediate reaction was that it was too brightly coloured for a true depiction of the Edinburgh scene. So, indeed, it was. But I think Miss Kay would have felt very happy about the imposed bright colours. She loved colours. She taught us to be aware of them. She could never accept drab raincoats. 'Why make a wet day more dreary than it is? We should wear bright coats, and carry blue umbrellas or green.' (In those days umbrellas were universally black or brown.) She said, 'I would like to see a grey coat and skirt for the spring, girls, worn with a citron beret. Citron means lemon, it is yellow with a sixteenth or so of blue. One would wear a citron beret in Paris with a grey suit.' We painted the primary, secondary and tertiary colours. I believe that, with Miss Kay, colour came before drawing or form. To her, colour *was* form. 'Rossetti knew well how to use the complementary tertiary colours, russet and olive green.' And she showed us the picture of Dante's encounter with Beatrice painted with russets and greens. I don't believe she cared much about Dante or Beatrice or the narrative element in the picture; it was simply a colour-fest. 'You will always know Corot', she said, 'by his small touch of red, such as a hat. That makes the painting.'

We could have begun to learn the arts and sciences of colours elsewhere, it is true; Miss Kay's lessons probably did not differ in substance from anyone else's. What filled our minds with wonder and made Christina Kay so memorable was the personal drama and poetry within which everything in her classroom happened. Her large, dark eyes were always alert and shining –

that, I think, was half of the magic. Shapes and sculptures, arithmetical problems, linguistic points moved easily around each other. Part of our curriculum was the roots of our language. She would often stop in mid-sentence to point out a Latin, Greek or Anglo-Saxon root. I can see her, now, chanting:

> 'Merrily, merrily, shall I live now
> Under the blossom that hangs on the bough –

'And the root of "bough" is?'

Up would go a few hands.

'Right. *Bog*, to bend. It describes the flexible bough. Well, as I was saying, Ariel symbolizes freedom ... '

In *The Prime of Miss Jean Brodie* I said that Miss Brodie pointed out to us (as Miss Kay so often did) that 'educate' derives from the Latin *e* (out) and *duco* (I lead). She had strong views on education. She believed it was a 'leading out' of what was there already (I believe this is basically an Aristotelian theory) rather than a 'putting in'. When I saw the play of *Miss Brodie* I was puzzled and a little amused to see that another character was made, seriously, to put Miss Brodie right on this question: the right derivation was *educare*. Either the adaptor or one of the producers had not realized that the root of *educare* is *e* and *duco*. I was so pleased with the play as a whole that I didn't venture to point this out. I didn't want to nit-pick. And besides, I had the distinct impression that my views, as author of the book, were not really welcome.

Did Miss Kay have a sweetheart in her life? I think she did, long before our time. I would put her age at about fifty in my memory, and, looking at the class photograph, I think that is about right. The two years I was in Miss Kay's class, the last classes in the junior school, were 1929 and 1930. She was of the generation of clever, academically trained women who had lost their sweethearts in the 1914–1918 war. There had been a terrible carnage. There were no men to go round. Until we ourselves grew up there was a veritable generation of spinsters. At any rate, Miss Kay told us how wonderful it had been to waltz in those long full skirts. I sensed romance, sex.

There was no mistaking the romantic feminine ardour with which Miss Kay recounted her visit one summer, with two other ladies, to Egypt. Miss Kay described to us one of the dresses she wore on the cruise that bore her there – large red poppies on a black background, 'how right for my colouring'. And the visit to Egypt was recounted in every detail; we smelled the smells and felt the heat. We saw the tall, dignified figure of the guide (the dragoman, as he was called) and sensed Miss Kay's attraction to him. While discussing with her the different Lord's days (Friday for the Muslims, Saturday for the Jews, Sunday for the Christians) the dragoman said, with a spiritual smile, 'Every day is the Lord's day.' This impressed Miss Kay greatly, as did his appearance at the railway station when she and her two travelling companions left the country; he bore for each a large bunch of flowers. When I repeated this exotic tale to my mother, she remarked that Thomas Cook (the main travel agent of those days) paid for those flowers. I felt that this was dreadfully cynical, but I couldn't help feeling at the same time that my mother was probably right, and we had a laugh together about it.

I have said Christina Kay was a devout Christian. She knew how to apply her Christianity. For instance, she felt 'Land of Hope and Glory' was basically anti-Christian. And we were expressly forbidden to join in any singing of the lines 'Wider still and wider Shall thy bounds be set; God who made thee mighty, Make thee mightier yet.' Of course, she was quite right. Such teachings, the sheer logic of the contradiction inherent in them to the moral culture we honoured, sank in. Miss Kay recommended to us, instead, the lines of Kipling's 'Recessional': 'The tumult and the shouting dies; The captains and the kings depart; Still stands thine ancient sacrifice; An humble and a contrite heart.' More than once, Miss Kay brought home to our attention exactly *what* we were singing so lustily. We were taught not to be carried away by crowd emotions, not to be fools.

Miss Kay's scriptural lessons were among her most marvellous. She had a true sense of the poetry of the Bible. Before reaching her class, we had been taught the Scottish catechism. I loved the beginning:

Q. What is man's chief end?
A. Man's chief end is to glorify God and enjoy Him forever.

We also knew the Ten Commandments.

At some stage before I came to Miss Kay's class, when I was about nine, I had a kind of religious experience. I saw a road-workman knocked down or hit by a tram-car. He ran from the spot with his arms spread out and fell beside the pavement. I saw this from a place where I was playing with some other children from school. We were all speedily ushered out of the way, and so I had no means of knowing if the man had been injured, or maybe electrocuted, or if he lived or died. My father could find nothing about it in the evening paper. But the image of the workman with arms outspread stayed in my mind for a long time. I fancied he had gone to Heaven, and imagined him there in his workman's cap and overalls. I thought he liked me. I spoke to nobody about him.

This image stayed with me for at least two years; then I ceased to be 'haunted' by my workman. I remembered only how he once had been in my mind.

I flourished at my Scripture lessons in Miss Kay's class, she so well illustrated and explained the symbolism of both the Old Testament and the New. She made us learn the great passages by heart – the prophecy of Isaiah 53 ('Who hath believed our report?'); I Corinthians 13 on Charity ('Though I speak with the tongues of men and of angels'); the song of Deborah; the song of Miriam; the Beatitudes; the Annunciation; the song of Simeon. I can recite them still.

At least twice a week after school, I would go to the public

63

lending library in Morningside; it has been built on the site of a former schoolhouse. I had lots of tickets that entitled the borrower to take out books—my own and my mother's, and also my father's when Philip didn't need them for his studies. I would bring home four books at a time, most of them poetry, for I was destined to poetry by all my mentors. Nineteenth- and twentieth-century poets were my preference – Wordsworth, Browning, Tennyson, Swinburne, and what were known as the Georgian poets (we were in the reign of George V): Edmund Blunden, Rupert Brooke, Walter de la Mare, Yeats, John Masefield, Robert Bridges, and, the only woman among them, Alice Meynell. I was always discovering new poems for Miss Kay to read. 'Have you read this? Look at that,' I would say. I was a passionate admirer of Masefield's narrative verse, especially *The Dauber* and *Reynard the Fox*. It was while I was in Miss Kay's class that I read *Jane Eyre*, and Mrs Gaskell's *Life of Charlotte Brontë*, and *Cranford*. I also tackled George Eliot's *The Mill on the Floss*, without much success.

Miss Kay took Frances and me to the theatre and to concerts, sometimes to a good film, paying out of her own pocket. She begged us not to mention this to the other girls, 'lest they should feel it is favouritism'. Which of course it was. But she told the whole class that they were the *crème de la crème*, and meant it, because they were hers.

Amongst our clandestine treats with Miss Kay were visits to modern poetic plays. There was at the time a repertory theatre company called the Arts League of Service, which we felt was very romantic. It appealed to us that the actors went round the countryside to act in small towns, sometimes sleeping in barns.

Miss Kay realized that our parents' interest in our welfare was only marginally cultural. She was determined that Frances and I should benefit from all that Edinburgh had to offer. We loved it. She felt rewarded by our response, as she told my mother years later. One of our special treats was going to hear John Masefield read his poems. This was around the time he became Poet

Laureate, in 1930, and his fame was at its height. In those years, a poet could draw an immense audience. Twenty years later, when I wrote a book about Masefield, I recorded that event:

On this occasion Mr Masefield read parts of *Dauber* – the passage on the rounding of Cape Horn. I remember particularly how well *Minnie Marlow's Story* came over. His voice was remarkable. When he began to read everyone was aware that the poet was not shy, after all. He read like a true bard. Since then, I have heard many bards reading their own verse; most are diffident, some try to overcome this by over-dramatizing. I have not heard anyone read his own work like John Masefield, as if he believed in it. He read as he might have read someone else's work, and that is a very difficult thing for a poet to do. His pronunciation was very pure, his tones very clear.

The most exciting of these outings with our beloved Miss Kay was to the Empire Theatre to see Anna Pavlova, indisputably the world's greatest dancer of her time – an event mentioned in the letter from Frances which I have already quoted. Actually, this was Pavlova's last tour. The great ballerina died shortly afterwards. On this occasion, she danced *The Death of the Swan*. I remember the sinking swan, and the two final death taps of Pavlova's fingernails, on the floor of the stage, like claws. Frances and I were now twelve years old. Both had already seen ballet-dancing, but we had never thought such dancing as Pavlova's and her *corps de ballet*'s could exist. We spoke of it together time and again afterwards. We were busy, too, on various joint projects – nature stories and descriptions of life on Mars, and poems. What happened to those notebooks of ours? Who knows?

That year, I had a batch of five poems published in an anthology of young people's poems called *The Door of Youth*. I was one of the youngest contributors. This fact, and the number

65

of poems, drew some attention to them. They had a certain lyrical quality. There was a poem about time (in which I noted that 'as I write this verse on Time/that self-same Time is flying.'); one about a stag hunt (in which the stag gets away); a poem about the sea, in which it features as a ravenous lion preying on ships and, in another mood, as a horse; a poem against the snaring of rabbits and against fox hunting; and a poem 'To Everybody', which was used as the dedicatory item in the book.

My poems in the school magazine were often influenced by Miss Kay's lessons on relativity. One of the library books recommended by her was *The Mysterious Universe* by Sir James Jeans, a famous popular astronomer. I wrote poems about the universe, such as one in which the inhabitants of other planets 'Look up to the sky and say/"The Earth twinkles clearly tonight."' Miss Kay predicted my future as a writer in the most emphatic terms. I felt I had hardly much choice in the matter.

Christina Kay was an experimental teacher. Once, she separated us according to our signs of the zodiac: she had read somewhere that children of the same zodiacal sign had a special, mysterious affinity. For a time I was separated from Frances, a Capricorn, and put beside a boring Aquarian. What happened as a result of this experiment was nothing. But even that nothing Miss Kay somehow made into an interesting, a triumphant discovery.

Her father had died when she was still a girl. It had fallen to her to manage affairs for her widowed mother. She told us of the day she had to go and query a bill at the Edinburgh gas office. Our class of girls, incipient feminists, was totally enthralled by Miss Kay's account of how the clerks tittered and nudged each other: a *female* desiring to discuss the details of a gas bill! 'But', said Miss Kay, 'I went through that bill with the clerk, point by point. He at first said he couldn't see any mistake. But when I asked to see the manager he had another look at the bill. He consulted with one of his colleagues. Finally he came to me with a very long face. He admitted there had been an error in calculation. I made them amend the bill, and I paid it then and there. *That*', said Miss Kay, with her sweet, wise smile, 'taught them to sneer at a businesslike young woman.'

Miss Kay always had the knack of gaining our entire sympathy, whatever her views. She could tolerate, even admire, the Scottish aristocracy (on account of their good manners), but the English no. She made a certain amount of propaganda against English dukes, who, she explained with the utmost scorn, stepped out of their baths every morning into the waiting arms of their valets, who stood holding the bath-towels and who rubbed them dry. This made us all laugh a lot. And, in fact, we often had cause for general mirth in Miss Kay's class.

After school, Miss Kay was an ardent lecture-goer. She attended lectures on such subjects as theology and German poetry, which were available to the general public at the University of Edinburgh. She went to lectures on health and 'care of the hair and hands' at some other institution. She went to hear art historians and educationalists. And on Sundays she would generally be at Professor Tovey's Sunday concerts in the Usher Hall. (Professor Donald Francis Tovey was Edinburgh's leading musicologist and conductor.) All these events, like her summer, Easter and Christmas holidays, Miss Kay would bring back to school to offer up to us and enrich our lives.

A correspondent has sent me a note from John Steinbeck's tribute to great teachers, which I think applies well to Christina Kay:

> I have come to believe that a great teacher is a great artist and that there are as few as there are any other great artists. Teaching might even be the greatest of the arts since the medium is the human mind and spirit.

I continued to enjoy a certain fame as the school's poet. I should describe at this point the curious and ambiguous experience I had after leaving Miss Kay's class when we all moved to the Higher Grade, as the senior school department was called. It was 1932, the year of the centenary of the death of Sir Walter Scott. A poetry competition was launched among the schools of Edinburgh by the Heather Club, a men's club founded in 1823 (for what purpose I do not know, except that it was very Scottish). I won first prize with my poem about Sir Walter Scott, and another girl at Gillespie's got third prize. The school was doubly jubilant; everyone was delighted. So delighted that I hadn't the heart, I couldn't possibly explain how I felt about the prize itself. Partly, it was a number of books, and that pleased me. But partly it was a coronet, with which I was to be crowned Queen of Poetry at some public Scott-centenary celebration. My mother was overjoyed, as was nearly everyone else, in school and out of school. I felt like the Dairy Queen of Dumfries, but I endured the experience and survived it. A star actress, Esther Ralston, did the crowning. It was a mystery to me what she had to do with poetry or Sir Walter Scott. The coronet itself was cheap-looking, I thought. The only person who openly agreed with my point of view was our reserved and usually silent headmaster, T.J. Burnett. He knew I had to go through with it now that I had won the prize, but he showed a sense of the unsuitable nature of this coronet affair. He was essentially an administrator, a man of very few words. 'Tinsel,' he said quietly to me, and then he made a congratulatory speech in front of the school. According to his daughter, Maida, he remarked at home, 'That lassie can write.' I know he was indignant for me. After the event, Miss Kay paid us a visit in the upper school with a press cutting in her hand. She said nothing to belittle the affair. But she did say, as she held up the photograph to the class, 'You can see the sensitivity in that line of Muriel's arm.' And, indeed, you can see an involuntary shudder in the line of my arm in the picture.

Frances, on this occasion, made me a small 'laurel wreath' of coloured wax, which I still treasure. With it she gave me a verse that she had composed for me:

Though on fame's dizzy heights you stand,
Though you climb ladders without end,
Please don't forget me for I am
Your dear and most devoted friend.

Fairly recently, I had occasion to remind Frances about these lines; I was also able to add that 'fame's dizzy heights' are more often than not a great pain in the neck.

One of the good effects of this event on me was my meeting with the adjudicator of the prize, Lewis Spence, an Edinburgh poet and considerable man of letters. The classics teacher Anna Munro (known as Beanie) and I went to tea with him at his home the Sunday after the awful ceremony. Lewis Spence was the first professional writer I had met. We talked about poetry, the essential suitability of certain forms and rhythms to certain themes. The conversation was general. I thoroughly enjoyed it. Some members of his family joined us, dispensing tea. Lewis Spence said to me, 'Of course you will write as a profession.' His daughter, very languid and beautiful with long hair, played the guitar and sang 'La Paloma'. On the way home Beanie Munro said, 'She made "La Paloma" sound quite original, hackneyed as it is.'

What good times Frances and I had together! I went with Frances to Crail, a seaside town in Fife, to stay at her grandmother's house for part of the summer holidays. The North Sea was clean in those days but not always hospitable because of its wildness. We would sit on the shore and watch the steel-grey and white-foam breakers tossing the little shipping vessels far away.

At weekends we roamed in the botanical gardens, or went for walks at Puddocky (a puddock is a frog) beside the Water of Leith, then home to tea. We buried a document – I think it was a jointly written story – under an ancient tree in the botanical gardens. But what exactly it was, and why we buried it, I can't remember, except that I know it had a lot of the Celtic

Twilight culture woven into it. There was a room at the top of the school where the wind was especially rumorous. Frances and I called it the *Mary Rose* room. *Mary Rose* was a play by J.M. Barrie.

The year after Miss Kay's last class, when we were in the first forms of the upper, or senior, school, we were fully occupied in coping with our new variety of subjects; each one was taught in a different classroom by specialist teachers many of whom went around with their academic gowns floating from their shoulders. We dashed from class to class. We were now also in different houses, of which there were four: Gilmour, Roslin, Spylaw and Warrender. I was in Warrender, Frances in Roslin. It made no difference to our friendship; the system of houses applied predominantly to sports: hockey, tennis and swimming. (Which house would win the shield?) But Frances and I sat together in class as usual.

Alison Foster (nicknamed Fossil) was an enthusiastic and friendly English teacher who edited the school magazine. Beanie, Miss Munro, taught Latin and Greek; she was pale and quiet and fairly young.

There were a few male teachers. Mr Wishart was our singing master; he got tunefulness out of us, taught us the rudiments of music, and prepared us for our annual Gilbert and Sullivan show and for our concert in the Usher Hall. There, after the prize-giving, a choir of at least seven hundred girls in white dresses and black stockings rendered many a rousing number, to the apparent pride and delight of our parents and their friends. We ended with Blake's 'Jerusalem', accompanied on the organ by Herbert Wiseman, Edinburgh's organist No. 1.

The handsome art master, Arthur Couling, expressly admired my poems, but about my drawings he was expressly silent. Coolie, as he was called among the girls, was himself a practising artist. He had some successful shows; one of his paintings, with the tantalizing title 'Le Bateau à la Moustache Jaune', was bought by the Glasgow Corporation for the McLellan Gallery in

Glasgow. Dishy Arthur Couling also painted the scenery for our dramatic performances and our light operas.

Frances lived near Coolie's house; it was in Northumberland Street. We had such a 'pash' on Coolie, the infinitely glamorous, that we would walk up and down the street, quite unnecessarily, in the hope of catching sight of him. But Coolie's favourite girl was Betty Mercer, bold and clever, slightly anarchic, and very handsome. At the school dance he sat and talked to her all evening. He didn't dance with Betty, just talked. When we asked her what they had talked about, she said, 'Cosmetics.'

Once, when we were exasperating Coolie by our chatter in class, he said, 'If you girls don't shut up I'll smash this saucer to the ground.' The saucer was held high: he was trying to demonstrate the nature of an ellipse. We didn't quite shut up, so he smashed the saucer to the ground as promised. We were thrilled and astonished. I used this incident in *The Prime of Miss Jean Brodie*.

The history master, Mr Gordon, whom we called Jerry, was a short, fair man. I remember well his passion for the industrial revolution. The innocence of our minds and the universal decency of our schoolteachers' comportment can be gathered from the fact that he used to make me sit at the front of the class so that he could stroke my hair while teaching, without anyone thinking at all ill of him. The girls tittered quite a lot. I liked it quite a lot. There was nothing whatsoever wrong with Jerry Gordon. My former schoolmate, Elizabeth, has reminded me that when he saw that someone was not paying sufficient attention Jerry threw a piece of chalk at her. As Elizabeth remarks, this livened up the class. (When war broke out years later all the male teachers joined up, but Jerry, being over-age, remained, still throwing his chalk, according to reports.)

The Greek class was extra-curricular. Only three girls took Greek. We had to get to school at eight in the morning to fit in this extra lesson from Beanie Munro. I loved crossing the Links to school in the early morning, especially when snow had fallen in the night or was still falling. I walked in the virgin snow, making the first footprints of the day. The path was still lamplit, and when I looked back in the early light there was my long line of footprints leading from Bruntsfield Place – mine only. I loved the Bruntsfield Links in all seasons. In the long summer evenings of Scotland, I would practise on the Links putting green with my brother and his friends. Philip was a good and keen golfer. I would often follow him around the Links golf course for nine or even eighteen holes, helping to hunt for lost balls; and when I was old enough I took round the course my junior-sized set of three essential cleeks (clubs). These were a brassie, a mashie and a putter. Later, my brother gave me a driver and a niblick, the shafts of which my father cut down to size for me.

Miss Forgan (Forgie) taught French. She never appealed to me. She was a large-boned woman of late middle age. She would come into the classroom wearing an invisible crown of thorns and heaving an aggrieved sigh. Looking back over the years, I am convinced she was ill or – who knows? – perhaps burdened with family cares: an ailing father, a war-wounded brother. I would sometimes see her in the street after school, wearily hauling her shopping bags full of 'messages' that betokened a plural domestic life. I never offered to help Forgie with her shopping bags (as we were all brought up to do). I was afraid she would say no, nastily. Nevertheless, I did better at French with Forgie than I did with any other French teacher. This included the Mademoiselle who came from France to teach us for a year, and whom we were at great pains to follow. She spoke rapidly and volubly and was delighted with herself. She was very pretty. We were thoroughly dazed. Another French teacher was J.G. Glen, a mild man with white hair. He never taught me, but one of his pupils has since told me that once having learnt Mr Glen's French there was no possibility of ever pronouncing it right for the rest of one's life.

Mabel Marr, small and efficient, with her white coat, presided over the science room, alternating with Margaret Napier (Nippy), a highly qualified, rosy-cheeked woman, who also taught mathematics. So far I had been slow at arithmetic, but algebra and geometry appealed to me greatly, largely because of Miss Napier's teaching. For some odd reason, she showed faith in me, knowing me to be a poet. The result was that I got high marks in both science and mathematics. I still have my science book, in which we wrote up our guided 'experiments'. I loved the science room, with its benches and sinks, its Bunsen burners, its burettes, pipettes, test tubes, and tripod stands.

'Unless you specialize in chemistry or physics,' said Nippy, 'you will partially forget all this when you leave school. But as soon as you are reminded of any particular aspect it will come back to you.' She was right. In spite of the claptrap, when I look at my science book it comes back clearly to me that, following an experiment involving the burning of phosphorus in an enclosed space of air over water, the conclusion is: 'When a substance is burned in air (or tarnish is formed) one fifth of the air is used up. Therefore four fifths will be left. Hence the atmosphere consists of one fifth of active air (a gas able to combine readily with substances) and four fifths inactive air (a gas difficult to combine).' When I contemplate this in my schoolgirl handwriting, I see again the apparatus – bell jar, phosphorus, crucible lid, the trough, the water. I smell again the peculiar and dynamic smell of Gillespie's science room. Like all schoolchildren, we called our science lessons 'stinks'.

An alternative science and maths teacher was the wandlike Sandy Buchan, who impressed on us the dangers of trusting in appearances, especially where colourless, odourless and tasteless matter was concerned. He put to us the awful caution:

> Poor little Tommy Jones
> We'll see him no more,
> For what he thought was H_2O
> Was H_2SO_4.

73

I remember his enunciation of 'colourless, odourless and tasteless' in a precise Edinburgh voice. I reflected then, and still reflect, that there could be people like that: no colour, no taste, no smell. The moral is, avoid them; they might be poison. Sandy Buchan looked very elegant crossing the Links with his hat, gloves, walking-stick and long winter coat, but for sex appeal he couldn't compete with Coolie.

Another teacher who was under the impression that my bent for literature might add something to her class was Miss Anderson (Andie), who taught gym and dancing and was head games mistress. I was no good, really, at gym, and little better at dancing. As for games, I was what the hockey captain called 'one of the spectators'. But Andie would ask me to comment on our dancing, mostly folk dancing. She wanted me to give some imaginative life to it. Once, I was sitting cross-legged on the floor leaning against the parallel bars of the gymnasium and watching a group of girls performing a dance called 'The Mill' when Andie asked me what I thought of it. I can't recall exactly what I replied, except that it was an exercise in diplomacy. I stood up and said something about the dancing being lovely but the dance not: to represent a mill the tempo should be speeded up. I think that this satisfied Andie and that she made our accompanist play faster. Frances was a very graceful dancer. In fact, she grew up to be a tall beauty; it was rightly said she moved like a swan. And she always maintained her sweet nature.

Andie herself was an enormous, athletic-looking woman, yet very light on her feet. The girdle of her gym tunic was tied round her hips, as was the fashion then, and tied in a very precise bow. That girdle would have gone three times round the average woman's hips. Andie's features were regular, her hair marcel-waved. She would arrive at school in her own little black car, very sporting, wearing a dark leather coat. One of her pupils remembers how excellent she was as a Scottish folk dancer, participating in public performances in Princes Street Gardens. To my memory, her gymnastic feats would have been amazing

74

even if she had not had to heave around that large bulk. She seemed to have built-in springs like the new mattresses that were coming on the market in our parts.

Although I was not much support to my team at hockey, I had to put in some afternoons at our playing fields at Meggetland in south-west Edinburgh. I had a hockey stick that I had acquired cheaply from an older girl who had grown out of it. But I needed hockey boots. My father couldn't afford them; just at that moment he had bills to pay – no, hockey boots were impossible. I played in my ordinary walking shoes a few times, but very soon afterwards my father appeared one evening after work with a pair of second-hand hockey boots. They were a perfect fit. I was overjoyed, especially as those boots had a rather kicked-about and experienced look; they were not at all novices in the field. My father smiled round the room, delighted with his success.

Who was Blossom? For many years I could not remember her real name, until I was lately reminded by Dorothy (Forrest) Rankine. 'Blossom was to us Miss McLean, graduate of Edinburgh University, a formidable, white-haired, stately presence who used her black chalky gown to great effect as a Roman toga when she taught Latin with such dedication to us.' She also taught botany hence, I have always supposed, her nickname. And according to Jean Guild, another of Miss McLean's pupils, her nickname, Blossom, derived from her name Charlotte; this went from Apple Charlotte to Apple Blossom.

The Misses Kirkwood and Lynn taught sewing in those days before electric machines had reached the school. They both had pretty hands, which I much admired, but no style at all. The summer dresses they made us cut out and sew up were hideous, unwearable. The slippers we were induced to knit made one look like Minnie Mouse. Still, Frances and I filled in the sewing period, three-quarters of an hour a week, with quiet conversations about the poetry we were writing. Quiet, though not whispered, conversations were encouraged in the sewing class, for we sewed in pairs.

John Brash also taught science. He was young and fairly good-looking, but we thought him, in our jargon, 'a Jessie'. This does not mean homosexual in Scotland; it means slightly effeminate.

According to Jean Guild he was susceptible to the girls. Another correspondent from those days of old, Dorothy L. Forrester, writes that there was more to him than met the eye. Dorothy Forrester tells an anecdote about a reproduction of the Degas dancer bending over to tie her shoe being objected to by some puritanical colleague because of its view of the girl's behind. This picture, on a wall outside John Brash's lab, was eventually removed by the headmistress whereupon another colleague said to Mr Brash, 'I hear you've lost your *derrière de Degas*.' 'But I've still got my *arrière-pensée*.'

John Brash never married. He is now in his nineties, still flourishing.

When the staff annually played the school's first hockey eleven, how vigorous they all were. How they pounded down the field, waving their sticks, especially Coolie and large, lusty, red-haired Mr Tate, a maths teacher. The staff players sometimes slipped and fell on the muddy field, to the heartless applause and ironic encouragement of the onlookers assembled round the edge. Andie led the staff team, sometimes to glory. ('Go it, Nippy!' 'Well saved, Andie!')

It was sixty years ago. The average age of those high-spirited and intelligent men and women who taught us was about forty; they were in their prime. I cannot believe they are nearly all gone, past and over, gone to their graves, so vivid are they in my memory, one and all.

I think we enjoyed an advantage over boarding-school pupils in our well-organized and friendly day school. We had the benefit of a parallel home life, equally full of daily events, and the impinging world of people different from our collegiate selves.

Comparing our young youth with the lives of teenagers over

the intervening years, Frances has lately written to me, 'We had the best life, Muriel.' In spite of the fact that we had no television, that in my home at least we had no electricity all during the 'thirties (only beautiful gaslight), that there were no antibiotics, and no Pill, I incline to think that Frances is right.

CHAPTER THREE

We got out of school between three thirty and four in the afternoon and started our parallel life at home in the Edinburgh of the late 'twenties and early 'thirties of this century. In the aspiring Morningside district where cleanliness and godliness shook hands with each other, honesty was the best policy, all was not gold that glistered and necessity was the mother of invention. Nobody questioned these maxims; we had from them a sense of security which the precarious economic position of the country could not shake. The times were, however, decidedly shaky.

In May 1926, when I was eight years old, there had been a general strike in Britain which lasted nine days. Our school did not close but some children could not attend through lack of transport. The motives and social background of the strike had been fully explained to us by our teachers, who I incline to think were on the workers' side, although they were officially impartial. However that may be, we all had felt the shivery possibility of a revolution.

That summer of 1926 was the last year in which my mother came to meet me from school. After that, I was old enough to make my way home alone. But sometimes on fine days my mother would bring her knitting and sit with other mothers on a bench in the lovely park that was Bruntsfield Links.

With my schoolmates I joined in ritualistic outdoor games

that I was soon to grow out of. We had many variations of skipping games. To whirl the skipping rope was to 'caw' it.

> Raspberry, strawberry, gooseberry tart
> Tell me the name of your sweetheart.

The answer was A, B, C, etc. until the appropriate initial was mentioned and the skipping girl fell out. She then revealed the boy's name.

There was a ring game for girls and boys, often played at children's parties, but also outdoors. It was both innocent and sexy. A girl stood in the centre of a dancing ring.

> Here's a poor widow who's left alone
> She has no one to marry upon.
> Look to the east and look to the west
> And choose the one that you love best.

The dancing stopped. The boy who happened to be opposite the girl in the centre, joined her.

> Now they're married we wish them joy,
> Every year a girl or a boy.
> Loving each other like sister and brother
> We pray the couple to kiss together.

Which they did, to the frank applause of all onlookers. We bowled hoops along the pathways and spun tops.

Counting our parents we were 'four of a family', as my father used to say. My brother Philip was interested in science. In the 1950s Philip emigrated to the United States, to become a research chemist in the Navy Department and, with his family, a US citizen. He is now retired in San Diego, and writes from there his reminiscences of our annual holidays to our mother's home in Watford in Hertfordshire. Philip remembers:

... how I used to put all the chairs together in the hallway like a train weeks before we went. Such a build-up of excitement until the eventful day came and we got a cab down to the Caley [Caledonian] Station. Mother would make sandwiches for the trip – eggs and cress and sometimes ham and fruit and of course her bottle of wine. The most amazing thing was, before the train started to go Mother would be giving our sandwiches to any other people in the carriage, so that by the time we got to Carstairs, all the food was gone and we had to wait until we got to Crewe to get a cup of tea from the wagon that came around. Then on to Stafford and Rugby and the excitement grew as we entered Watford Tunnel, and I knew that it wouldn't be long before we arrived at Willesden Junction and on to Bushey and Oxhey where Grandfather was awaiting our arrival. I always liked Watford with its market-town atmosphere and its closeness to London. We used to go on many picnics to Hemel Hempstead, Croxley Green, St Albans, etc. and of course a special day set aside for a visit to London on top of the bus, and to Petticoat Lane.

Trains in those days were steam-driven, with a stoker to keep the fire burning all during the night. (Ours was an eight-hour journey.) Before our departure the station was filled with smoke, stinging our eyes. The guard, armed with a red flag and a green, would finally wave the green. He would blow his whistle. Then the train would be off, but only after numerous grunts and unbalancing jerks. At every stop a man with a lantern and an iron mallet would come examining and sounding the train's steel joints and wheels with loud, and yet comforting, clanks in the night.

Our holidays in Watford form the basis of my story 'The Gentile Jewesses' which is nearly factual, but in which I have written mainly about my grandmother, Adelaide. A high-spirited character, she was rather plain compared with my red-haired grandfather, Tom Uezzell, who was reputed to

81

be fifteen years her junior.

Tom's parents had been corn dealers of Watford. He was tall and stooping; his well-worn country jacket hung loosely from his shoulders; his trousers were dark grey and baggy at the knees. I never saw him dressed in anything else but those old clothes, in which, however, he had a casual, superior look. Visibly, he loved my grandmother, following her everywhere with his eyes. Uezzell is a rather rare old English name, deriving from French. In Watford I had a great many Uezzell connections, and one of the streets was called Uezzell Close.

My parents put everything they could into making our annual holiday fun for us and for themselves. My happiest memories are country walks with my grandfather who could name every bird, even by its call, and every plant or flower. We would cross running streams on stepping-stones only, and later Grandfather would be blamed for my wet feet. His names for me were Canary or Ladybird. My grandmother, who kept the village shop, bustled about all morning and reposed all afternoon.

Watford has now spread and sprawled. It is no longer a market town. The old High Street where at No. 288 my grandmother kept shop, is now on the margin of the town. I went back to Watford a few years ago. It has happened to me three times in my life that I have revisited a place where I have stayed to find that the house was only just in course of reconstruction or, as in the case of my grandmother's shop, and the house where we spent our holidays, had been newly demolished. The two other houses in that little part of the street were still standing. For some reason, on the site of the demolished building someone had planted a row of roses. They were young plants and looked as though they were freshly placed. It was mysterious to me to see those roses flourishing on the place where my grandparents flourished, kept shop, brought up their children and welcomed their grandchildren. The flowers seemed to have been planted in their honour, but this was a fantasy – my grandparents were dead so long ago, and other tenants had taken their place. On that day I could almost hear my grandfather's voice again, as he mounted the creaky stairs with a cup of morning tea in his hand. 'Wake up, Canary!'

Another discovery that moved me was that one of the remaining houses was still, on the street floor, a newsagent and tobacconist shop as it had been in the days when my father used to go along there for his 'ten Players' each day. It was so unchanged externally – almost the same advertisements lining the outside walls – that I went inside on a pretext. I fancied that the counter had changed position but that was all. Obviously there were living quarters at the back of the shop and upstairs. Identical with my grandparents' house, the garden at the back could be seen through two windows from the street. The young woman who served me had only newly taken over with her husband. She knew nothing of the people who had lived in the demolished house where roses were planted.

In my grandparents' day there was a privy attached to the house, but approached from outside. My brother showed me a hole in the wall of a scullery which gave on to the privy and, always ready to show off in front of me, his best audience, Philip got a broom and poked the handle through the hole. Whereupon my grandmother shot right out of there, loudly exclaiming, with a flurry of white petticoats.

My grandparents' parlance often retained some flavour of the eighteenth century. Adelaide Uezzell didn't go for a walk, she 'went abroad'. As she kept a shop and had little time for household chores she sent the bed and table linen out to be washed. My grandfather, Tom, referred to this as 'the larndry'. I have heard elderly English people pronounce it so well into the 1940s.

My hands stroked Flossie, my grandfather's golden spaniel. He also had a ginger cat that he loved. 'You've got carroty hair,' quipped my grandmother, 'and you've had carroty children and now you've got a carroty dog and a carroty cat.' My mother was the only dark-haired member of the family. All the rest of us were more or less 'carroty' including my Uncle Phil's six children, with whom we sometimes played on our Watford holidays.

Our great-aunts Nancy and Sally Uezzell lived in Vicarage Road, which I felt quite just, since 'vicar' was a key word in their universe. The vicar usually wormed his way into any discussion on any of the admittedly limited topics they discussed. Their house smelt of themselves uniquely – a mixture of carbolic soap and other cleaning materials of the age, such as black lead (for the stove and the grate in the fireplace), beeswax for the woodwork, paraffin to mix with rotten-stone (powdered limestone) for the brass candlesticks and the door knockers, chloride of lime for bleaching linen, turpentine for mixing with the beeswax, vinegar for the rinsing-water and ammonia for God knew what. The punk arising from these lethal products clung to my great-aunts' clothes and hung around the curtains. To me, their tea-biscuits tasted of camphor mothballs.

My mother took her aunts flowers from her father's garden. They were set aside for the altar.

Sally was the succubus of Nancy. For evidence of this I have only my strong childhood intuition, and various inferences to be drawn from my elders' comments. Sally would have been nicer if she hadn't been with Nancy. I was definitely glad that I didn't 'belong' to that pair.

They were known to have disapproved of their brother Tom's marriage to Adelaide, but that was a thing of the past. Sally sat with her hands folded while Nancy did the talking, so mournful-sounding to me. It was she who was always the first to write and spread the news of any young lady in Watford who was pregnant before marriage. I remember my mother once remarking, on reading one of Aunt Nancy's letters, 'After all, it's only Nature.' These sisters were often described by the family as 'strait-laced', which was an image drawn from the tight-laced stays worn by the women of their time.

My mother was later to be really incensed by a notice inserted in the *Watford Observer* by Nancy, and proudly forwarded to us,

84

when my grandmother died at home with us in Edinburgh: 'After long suffering patiently borne she fell asleep in Jesus.' There followed a verse beginning, 'For now she wears a golden crown . . . ' My mother rightly objected to the 'long suffering' since my grandmother, although disabled by a stroke, did not suffer long or noticeably. We took great care of her. As for falling asleep in Jesus, it was a moot point.

My grandmother's father had been a Jew, her mother a Christian. During her lifetime she belonged to every new group in Watford whenever it was formed. She was a suffragette, marching for the women's vote. She belonged to the Church of England Mothers' Union and tried out both spiritualist and Methodist meetings. They were her only social occasions. When she died in Edinburgh the Watford Women's Church Union sent a gravestone which my mother placed on her grave. This was in a Jewish cemetery, so it was swiftly removed. Forty years later my son, who had never known her, put up a gravestone with Jewish wording to mark her resting place. My Uezzell cousins believe she was not of Jewish inheritance at all, which is at least correct in that Jews inherit religious identity through the mother. But I think she had a definite Jewish connection through her father, although most of her life was lived in a country environment of Christian churches and church events. It could be that there was a note of defiance in my great-aunts' claim in that newspaper notice, 'she fell asleep in Jesus', which they sent to my mother.

In Watford we used to go to the fair. I remember a tall Indian in a turban. (My mother doubted he was an Indian. She said he had covered his skin with walnut juice.) He was a phrenologist and read my brother's 'bumps'. This process consisted of pressing his hands all over my brother's skull. His fee was a shilling. I forget what glamorous future he predicted for Philip but I recall that he looked at my hands and said I would be musical. I noted how satisfied my parents were for their shilling's-worth.

In September when we took our annual holidays the blackberries would be thick in the hedgerows. We picked basketfuls, taking them home for jam-making. My grandmother's neighbours would pass by with bags of plums and apples from their trees, figs and apricots. My grandfather would put on long boots to wade into the river where there was a watercress bed, and bring it home in bunches; he grew raspberries and vegetables. It was he who made the butter for the household, by whisking and churning from a jug of thick cream, fresh from a friendly neighbouring cow.

I was in my eighth year when, on the death of my grandfather, our idyllic annual holidays at Watford came to an end. A curious event preceded my grandfather's death which made a great impression on me. We had on the wall of our kitchen above the fireplace an enlarged photographic portrait of a patriarchal type of man from my father's family. I don't know who he was apart from the fact that he was not a relation, and for that reason I often wondered what he was doing there. Perhaps he was some famous professor or rabbi, held in esteem. One evening the picture fell. No one was hurt, but the glass was shattered. My mother was distressed. She said it was a bad omen. I think she was worried about her father being ill with bronchitis at the time. Sure enough, there came a wire next day, summoning my parents to Watford; in fact my grandfather died of pneumonia shortly before their arrival. The patriarch was never replaced on the wall.

This was the second death in the family in my experience. The first had been some years earlier when my mother's younger brother, Harry, died of the effects of poison gas to which he had been exposed in the trenches during the First World War. I remember my Uncle Harry only as being first young and merry, next, suddenly thin, bent and ghost-like and very soon afterwards not there at all. He was buried in Edinburgh in a Church of Scotland graveyard at Corstorphine. Some of my father's sisters accompanied his wife, Bessie, and my parents to the funeral; they came afterwards to our house, wearing black clothes.

Bluebell

My grandmother shut up her shop that summer. We went all four to fetch her; she came to live with us in Edinburgh for the last four years of her life. My mother and I helped her to pack. What fascinated me most about this operation was the vast difference between her clothes and ours. To begin with there were flannel garments worn against the skin winter and summer, which my grandmother called 'my chemises'. Then came frilly tops, 'my bodices', to be followed by 'my stays' which were flexible corsets inset with whalebone and laced, criss-cross, with tape to pull in the waist-line. Next, 'my drawers' which had long legs to below the knees and no gusset, so that the 'private regions' had no covering at all. These drawers were frilly with elaborate hand-made tucks and pale-coloured ribbons tying them together under the knees and at the waist. 'My petticoats' were voluminous, gathered at the waist; one in each set was cream-coloured or grey flannel, one was white linen edged with lace and one was black. My grandmother's stockings were black wool. They were kept up by pink elastic bands, her garters. 'My night-shifts' were white flannel for winter, cotton for summer, spacious, with high necks and long sleeves, very frilly. I had the impression, which I believe is correct, that all these numerous garments had been in use for a very long time, perhaps twenty or thirty years or more. Perhaps since her marriage. They were well cared for, the cotton starched and ironed; there were neat little patches here and there on these clothes, and darns that were works of art in themselves.

One group of objects puzzled me. They were cotton bags about six inches square, attached to long tapes. It was explained that these were pockets. My grandmother had her pocket tied round her waist between the top petticoat (the black one) and the skirt of her dress. This meant that to get anything out of her pocket my grandmother had to heave up her skirt to the knees and thrust her hand into this mysterious hanging bag (from which she frequently produced a piece of chocolate for us).

Among the garments we helped to pack was an intriguing item of underwear which my grandmother wore seldom, and only in deep winter. It was called combinations. It was an all-in-one wool suit with knee-length leggings and wrist-length sleeves, and, like the drawers, it had no gusset. These were very 'modern' to my grandmother. They belonged to that generation of young ladies one of whom is described by T.S. Eliot in *The Waste Land*, as drying her combinations on the window sill.

During the time my grandmother stayed with us she never acquired any new clothes. Her outer wear was far less abundant than her underwear. She had four dresses. They all came in two pieces, a bodice and a skirt. The bodice hooked together with a strong but invisible hook-and-eye arrangement. The skirt hooked at the side. It was gathered at the waist and went over at least two of the petticoats, depending on the season. Also depending on the time of year was the colour of the dress. For everyday wear, my grandmother wore a silver-grey dress in summer, a black woollen dress in winter. Her skirts reached to just above the ankles, a concession to the times when young women were already wearing knee-length skirts. For any evening parties or special occasions she wore a black satin dress heavily beaded with jet. Glittering-black jet formed my grandmother's favourite jewellery although she also wore a gold chain and locket with a picture of my grandfather in it.

In her clothes-trunk she had a pair of slippers, a pair of house shoes and a pair of black ankle boots for walking abroad. The other items of personal use were largely embroidered handkerchiefs, a case to hold them, and various pincushions.

But I have kept Bluebell to the last. Bluebell was what I called my grandmother's lovely blue silk brocade going-away dress the colour of cornflowers. I have never seen anything quite so beautiful, nor touched anything so sensuous before or since. When she came to us, Adelaide had no thought of ever wearing it again. She must have had her small, plump, Queen Victoria-like figure when she was married, about 1876, for it was still her right size. The reason I called this magnificent garment Bluebell is that a few years earlier, around 1923, she had written to tell my mother that she had been to a fancy-dress evening party at the Watford Church Union. She had gone dressed up as 'Bluebell' in her rich blue brocade gown, having arranged for a hat to be made with imitation bluebells laid on the brim, and a basket on her arm to be filled with the same fabric flowers. Adelaide Uezzell won a prize for the ensuing appearance, consisting of a two-pound jar of fig jam and a cherry cake. And so, when we packed the famous Bluebell dress in my grandmother's chest, and unpacked it again in Edinburgh, I felt as if I were handling a real historic museum piece. Of course I tried it on, and although it was far too big, I swept around in it, thinking of all the parts I could take in period plays. Alas, after the death of my grandmother, when I was thirteen, I succumbed to the current fashion and, with my mother's approval, cut up the Bluebell gown to make cushion covers. They looked wonderful, but the dress itself should never have been touched. It glowed with its deep and heavy brocaded blueness. It was sewn by hand, with a minutely stitched lining.

The first three years of my grandmother's stay with us she was able to join in most of our family excursions and fun. She didn't go out in the evening. My parents, both hard workers, used to go out almost every evening, either to friends or to see a film. My grandmother would be in bed by seven in the evening, and so I would often be left alone with her. I would usually be reading or studying while my grandmother snoozed or listened to the radio, which we called the wireless. This was a wonder to my grandmother. We had progressed from those early days when, in my infancy, my brother had constructed our first wireless, a crystal set. Our present 'set' was a Pye radio on which we could get the BBC and even some foreign stations. Philip, who was also studying, made tea or Ovaltine for us at about nine o'clock. By ten we were all in bed.

Earlier in the 'twenties my Auntie Gertie had emigrated to Australia to be married to her elder sister Lena's brother-in-law. We had letters from her, full of scenic effects. We also heard from the United States from our old friend Professor Andrew K. Rule. One of his letters told of his wife Charlotte's death. My mother cried bitterly at the news.

Towards the beginning of the 'thirties, Andrew Rule wrote suggesting that my father emigrate with us all to join him in the United States and take up the job of chief engineer at Louisville Seminary, of which Professor Rule was the head. My parents, I know, had been tempted by this suggestion. But my mother's feeling for her family held her back. My parents also felt that such a move, although economically it would have been an obvious advantage, might disturb their children's education.

The advent of my grandmother meant that we were cramped for sleeping-space. From the time of my grandmother's arrival I had to give up my room. Night after night, for years, I made up my bed on a sofa and fell into a sweet, deep sleep. If anybody had told me then, at the age of eight, that I was under-privileged I would have thought them out of their minds. I knew that other girls had a room to themselves and, on the other hand, others had hardly a bed at all. The two facts, that some had and some hadn't, didn't clash in my mind. They chimed together like many other facts in the world around me, that now, looking back, I might find discordant.

My grandmother suffered a stroke about three years later. I was now eleven years old, discovering the delights of poetry and art through that wonderful teacher Christina Kay. My school-days were now extremely exciting, and some of my new awareness of life's possibilities entered my parallel home life. Just as Miss Kay and her colleagues were forming the basis of the future characters in my novel *The Prime of Miss Jean Brodie*, so my grandmother's new problems, created by her disabilities, made me acutely aware of old age, a condition of which of course I had been aware, hitherto, but which, up to now, had been totally outside our intimate family life. I think my experiences in minding and watching my grandmother formed a starting-point for my future novel, *Memento Mori*, in which the characters are all elderly people.

Before her stroke I had noticed how her memory worked. It came in snatches, vignettes. I was beginning to practise memories myself. When my grandmother talked of her sister, Kitty, gloating over her because she had finer clothes, I would egg on my grandmother: 'And then what did you say?' 'I just walked out of the room and I said, "Goodbye, Rotten Row."' I knew that Rotten Row was the famous 'Rue du Roi' in Hyde Park where rich people took their daily ride. I thought my grandmother extremely witty, and she knew she could make me laugh. The last time she was able to leave her bed and sit with us, when she left, helped by my mother, she unexpectedly said, 'Goodbye, Rotten Row.' We were all rather upset. She remembered her meetings with the suffragettes and the memorable day in Watford when she marched up the High Street for the women's vote. In practice of my own memories, I then deliberately recalled two years back when my cousin Violet (daughter of my father's sister, Sarah, a most amusing woman) danced at a benefit performance in the Caledonian Hotel. She was dressed, Maurice Chevalier style, in striped trousers, tail coat and top hat. Vi carried a walking-stick and wore ostentatious gloves which were part of the act as she sang,

> I'm Burlington Bertie
> I rise at ten thirty.
> I saunter along like a toff.

> I walk up the Strand
> With my gloves on my hand,
> And I walk back again with them off.

I checked this event with Vi very recently. Yes, she remembers perfectly giving that song-and-dance act. She was fifteen to sixteen years old at the time. I was eight.

I remembered back how our cat had kittens. I would have been about six at the time. My brother was unsure how the kittens had been born. I informed him that the mother 'did' them. How I got this phrase or what exactly I meant by it I didn't know. I only recalled, looking back a few years later, how mightily amused my mother was by the remark. When the kittens were ready to leave the mother we had no room for them all. What should we do with them? My brother Philip was told to take them to the vet and have them put away. But instead, he touted the kittens round the hotels of Edinburgh and sold them for one shilling each, thus ensuring a good home with plenty of food and mousing prospects for each cat. We were all impressed by Philip's four shillings. We agreed that the cats would be all the better treated because their new owners had paid for them.

It was about the fourth year of her stay with us that my grandmother had her stroke. This meant that she was in bed most of the day, although after a while we managed to get her up for a few hours in the afternoon. I would find my grandmother sitting in her chair when I got home from school at three thirty or four in the afternoon. She was put back to bed at five. She progressively lost her powers of relevant speech. I tried very hard to discern some logic in what she was saying, but I never succeeded in finding any secret clue. If she referred to my brother she might say 'dressing-table', or if I talked about my school she would comment that it was laryngitis. We were all convinced she knew what she meant; it was only that she couldn't get the word. From my own elementary experiments I found there was no symbolism involved, no rational connection between what she said and meant.

One day in fine weather we thought it would be lovely to take Grandmother for a ride in an open horse-drawn carriage such as she had been used to. We could have managed to walk her step by step down the one flight of stairs that separated us from the street door. My father went off to order the cab while my mother revealed the exciting programme to her mother, and I started to get out my grandmother's best black clothes. To our astonishment my grandmother panicked. She put up a resistance like a trapped animal, forming all sorts of sentences in hysterical tones. We dropped all preparations and calmed her down. Philip put his head round the door. 'We're going to take you to Cramond for tea, Grandmother.' Cramond was a charming fishing village outside Edinburgh, but my grandmother let forth another unintelligible protest. My father had to return to the cab-agency and cancel the trip. Finally, it emerged by small stages that my grandmother thought we were using this outing as a ruse to 'put her away' in a home. This had never been in question amongst us. In those days there were no national health services, and old people's homes existed only for the very rich and unwanted or the poor and destitute. We were all full of consternation that my grandmother should imagine we could treat her so badly. It made me realize how vulnerable the aged are. I think her inability to communicate gave her a sense of frustration, that the absence of exact information opened her mind to suspicions. Very often we had smiled at my grandmother's foibles and imaginings, but we didn't smile at this incident. It was difficult to recognize in her the former outspoken champion for the rights of women.

That was a terrible day for us, and especially for my mother who was a devoted daughter and keenly felt her mother's unjust reactions. But before long we came to realize my grandmother's mind was really going. When I was about twelve she had another stroke and was completely bedridden for nearly a year before she died. This involved heavy nursing on my mother's part.

Although my grandmother was physically incapable there were times when she was now more mentally alert than before.

My mother was fairly strong, but my grandmother was heavy. I often stood by as my mother lifted and eased my grandmother from the bed to the bedside 'commode', or wooden seat with a lid which opened to the convenience of a deep toilet-pot. I wanted to help my mother with this necessary chore because, unlike other problems involving physical effort, such as lifting trunks or moving heavy furniture, it wasn't something that could be coped with by my father or brother. My mother said that skill was more important than strength in this business of moving my grand-mother gently out of bed and back again. In fact, by watching my mother I came to manage it myself without any strain that I can remember. There were three basic movements: first, I put my arm under my grandmother's back and helped her to a sitting position in bed, somehow shifting the pillows to bolster her up while I operated the second phase, a swivelling movement of her legs, so that they dangled over the edge of the bed; third, and most difficult, was a sliding, and at the same time, swerving movement of my grandmother's body until she had shifted her seat from the bed to the commode. It was important that the commode should be aligned with the bed beforehand. Before the return journey to bed, I was able to smooth the sheets and puff up the pillows. When I described this in detail to a qualified nurse, years later, I was happy to know from her that what my mother and I had done by instinct was in fact the correct procedure.

From now on my mother was free to resume some of her evenings out with my father. If anyone had suggested that this nursing of my grandmother was beyond what a child of twelve should be expected to do I would have thought they were simply incapable of seeing my grandmother's point of view. I would have felt, obscurely, that they were my grandmother's enemy.

But my mother discouraged me from most forms of house-work, except occasional tidying-up. She had a theory that if you didn't know how to do it you wouldn't have to do it, and besides,

Bernard Camberg, Muriel's father

Adelaide Uezzell, Muriel's grandmother

Watford: the shop
of all sorts

Muriel's grandfather,
Tom Uezzell, her mother
(Cissy) and goat

Philip Camberg, Muriel's brother

MAUD KERR
Lyrical Soprano

Lyon Silver Challenge Trophy Winner
Concert Artistes' Association, London
B.B.C. Soloist, London

Specialist in Scottish Song

The soprano upstairs

Charlotte Rule
(née Brodie)

Part of Muriel's
juvenilia

XXXI

Verse

Verse! that flower amongst
the rocks,
Lamp, that when dark, lights
all.
I pray you give a thought
to verse,
When world by ways do
call.
"I will light the ways of
ignorance,
For ignorance is nought.
Think not for those who
make the verse;
But for the verse give
thought!"

XXXII

To Everybody

The Artist has canvas,
The Dreamer has dreams,
A book is the Scholars possession,
A viol an organ,
A fiddle, or harp,
Are the things which delight
the Musician.
The Scribe he has offices
Filled full with pens
And sits and writes all
the day through,
But I put zeal and
zest
In the thing I love best,
'Tis a verse which I give
up to you.

James Gillespie's Girls' School, Junior Class, 1930: Muriel Camberg (Spark), 3rd row, 2nd from right; Frances Niven (Cowell), 3rd row, 3rd from right; Miss Christina Kay, centre

Muriel aged 10

The *Windsor Castle*

(*Left*) Muriel in
Bulawayo

The Victoria Falls

Muriel with her
son, Robin

Esther, Robin's
nanny

Marie Bonaparte (Princess George of Greece)

Muriel aged 29

(*Above*) Robin Spark

(*Top right*) Sarah Camberg
(Cissy), Muriel's mother

Bernard Camberg (Barney),
Muriel's father

Christmas Humphreys
(Toby)

Sefton Delmer

Graham Greene

(*Left*) Dr Marie Stopes

Allington Castle; a Carmelite retreat

Muriel with Tiny Lazzari

Alan Maclean

Bluebell

there was plenty of time to learn 'later'. She herself was a good English cook; but cleaning bored her and she did the minimum necessary. Every week we had a helper to scrub and clean. One was Sarah Coutts who fascinated me with stories about her 'man' and how she wouldn't marry him lest he shouldn't treat her children right. The other, much later on, was charming Fanny Pagan.

There was a small writing-desk in my grandmother's room for me to use while I was minding her. It had a sloping leather-covered surface which opened flat, and numerous drawers for papers and secrets. I was always happy at a desk. There, while my grandmother dozed, I did my homework, wrote my poems, read the books that I had brought home from the public library earlier in the evening and wrote letters, usually to my best friend Frances Niven with whom I shared our schoolroom double-desk. Frances wrote letters to me; we would exchange them next day. We neither of us had a telephone in our house. Our letters were comments on the poetry we were reading or on ideas for our nature studies. Those evenings I spent minding my grand-mother were interspersed by evenings when our adored Miss Kay took us to a theatre or concert. On those evenings it was my mother who stayed at home to look after the failing old lady.

When my grandmother died, I remember being called to her room to witness her last moments. It was about 9 p.m. The doctor had just left. I had put my hair in curlers. For some reason I felt that this would be unseemly at a death-bed, so I took out the curlers and combed my hair before I went in. My grandmother was unconscious. There was a strange sound. My father said softly, 'It's the death rattle.' Something was happening in my grandmother's throat. Her eyes were closed. The rattle stopped. She gave a great sigh and died.

My sharpest memories of her went back before her illness, to when she was at Watford, full of perkiness, keeping her village shop. I thought of her dressing up as Bluebell. And I thought of how she dug in her deep pocket for the chocolate she always kept there for us. I remembered above all her sardonic, humorous and robust remarks when privately discussing certain of her neighbours with my mother. One day I had overheard a snatch of conversation between them which I was decidedly not supposed to hear. They were discussing someone's difficult matrimonial life. My mother asked a somewhat rhetorical question: how do you keep men happy? 'You have to feed 'em both ends,' said my grandmother. I was always struck by the fact that many of her pieces of popular wisdom were expressed in terse monosyllabic words.

From my grandmother's possessions I have inherited an amber-coloured embossed glass bread plate with 'Give Us This Day Our Daily Bread' inscribed round the edge and two little Chelsea-china rustic figures called 'fairings', because they were given away at a fair about the middle of the nineteenth century. When I look at these, I still see them clearly in the small china-cabinet in Watford in my grandmother's sitting-room where she kept her best things.

For Hallowe'en, Frances and I made a witches' room out of one of the basement rooms of her house at 8 Howard Place. I stayed overnight on occasions like this when we had something to celebrate or some parts in a play to rehearse. Hallowe'en was celebrated by a roaring fire in the handsome old fireplace of a room which must once have been a large kitchen or servants' hall in that thrilling house next door to Robert Louis Stevenson's birthplace (which was No. 10). I was familiar not only with No. 8 but also with the Stevenson house, by our time a museum. But I have also seen the house in my mature years. I think it altogether charming, possibly mid-Victorian, a town house in a row. Of course it had nothing of the more impressive Edinburgh architecture of Adam, the eighteenth-century lines of Stevenson's later home at Heriot Row, but to me, and to Frances, it was full of mystery and stimulants to the imagination such as the equivalent, next door, of the old room where, with the lights out, before a flickering fire, we were Hallowe'en witches.

My friend Frances always had an instinctive talent for arranging the 'atmosphere' of a room. Her Hallowe'en production, although decidedly low-budget, was a masterpiece of rolled-up rugs propped upright, looking at us in the firelight, and scarily-draped furniture. We sat in our black cone-shaped cardboard hats and ate roasted chestnuts by the fire. We chanted and incanted and read our wildest poems and stories to each other. I read a poem, 'The Gallop', which I thought suitable for the All-Hallows; I recently found it again in a long-lost book of my juvenilia, most of which I had composed on those nights when I minded my grandmother. I believe it was on that year's Hallowe'en that I also read aloud one of my first short stories, 'The Black Star'. I have a particular affection for the following extract:

'You mean blackmail?' Her eyes widened.
'Exactly.' Lawrence's tone was charged with significance.

My poetry was rather more sophisticated than my prose. I was deeply interested in rhythms and curious about what one could make them mean in poetry. My poem 'The Gallop' did indeed speed over the pages for five stanzas of which the following are a sample:

> Horses wild horses!
> Alive as they gallop
> In fury along!
> As they gallop and gallop
> And gallop along!
> And gathering speed,
> And faster and faster,
> Nor heeding disaster,
> All trying to lead.

97

And breathing is strong
As they gallop along,
As they gallop and gallop along.

Meadows and streamlets,
Fields full of clover,
Cows that turn slowly
And moo as they pass.
Cows that stand watching
and watching –
and watching –
Munching the cud,
Knee-deep in the grass.
Blinking from silly old lazy old eyes,
Gaze with surprise
Gazing at horses,
Living and spirited
Beautiful horses!
Spirited, beautiful horses!

At this time, too, I was reading the Border ballads so repetitively and attentively that I memorized many of them without my noticing it. The steel and bite of the ballads, so remorseless and yet so lyrical, entered my literary bloodstream, never to depart.

All during my childhood I was given dolls as presents by aunts and friends. I used them mainly as actors in plays which I improvised as I went along. I recall having a fixed idea about one of the dolls. For some reason it needed an outdoor coat and hood trimmed with fur to fulfil the assigned role, so I bothered my busy mother every day before I left for school to dress up this doll accordingly. I didn't expect her to do so because she apparently took no notice; but one day I found on coming home that my doll was dressed to order, with my mother putting the last stitches on it. What I remember most about this occasion was how touched I was by my mother's action. When I was twelve I got a miniature bicycle – that is to say, it was something rather more advanced than the usual child's 'fairy-cycle' as they called it, but not really adapted to riding through traffic, even though it had real blow-up tyres. My father paid three pounds five shillings for it, in three instalments. I used it on the pavements around our home and on the tarmac pathways of the Links and the Meadows. It was an exceptional bike. I found I could make up poetry and stories in my head as I whizzed along, ringing my bell to scatter such of the sauntering population, with their little dogs, as were in my way.

My mother continued to play the piano and my father to sing to her accompaniment. One of the simply sentimental but most truly haunting melodies was 'Sometimes', the words of which my mother wrote out for me forty years later. They are:

> Sometimes between long shadows on the grass
> The little truant waves of sunlight pass.
> My eyes grow dim with memories awhile,
> Thinking I see you, thinking I see you smile.
>
> And sometimes in the twilight gloom apart,
> The tall trees whisper, whisper heart to heart
> From my fond lips, the eager answers fall,
> Thinking I hear you, thinking I hear you call.

Outside of school, by the summer of 1929, I had made two new friends, Guy and Denis Fermie. Guy was about my age, Denis a little younger. They lived in Bruntsfield Avenue which was a street at right angles to ours. They therefore shared with us the grassy square which our back windows looked on to and which was for the private use of tenants in our blocks. Guy, Denis and I used to sit in the back green and talk, very often, on long summer evenings when my mother was at home to keep my grandmother company. The boys' father was an Indian doctor, their mother a Scot. They went to expensive day schools. They were my first male playmates, for my brother, more than five years my senior, had friends who were nearer his age. Guy was particularly interesting and gentle. The other neighbouring boys were generally more inclined to be rough – perhaps not intentionally, but they got carried away with their fights and their more hazardous games. Besides, there were different games for boys and girls. For instance, girls did not often spin tops; boys wouldn't look at skipping ropes. But the Fermie boys, Guy and Denis, didn't seem keen to play the known games of childhood. Guy was socially mature for his twelve years, courteous, amused, interested in any subject whatsoever, while Denis listened to his elder brother, fascinated by our talk. It was a ritual that we sat cross-legged facing each other in the middle of the green. We were a sort of oasis, but I am not quite clear why. I remember the Fermie brothers' alert, dark eyes and pale brown gleaming skins, and Guy Fermie's shy and diffident smile, his intelligence, as we talked of geography, sex, schools, people, money, flowers, and all things possible. I attributed his difference from the other boys to his Indian side, I think rightly. I lost sight of the Fermies later, during the 'thirties. I supposed they had moved house, but I often wonder what became of them.

To grow from childhood into adolescence, and live as a teenager in the 1930s of Edinburgh, was to be aware of social nervousness. There was no possible way of hiding it, even though Edinburgh was not the worst-hit of Britain's cities during the great depression of the 'thirties. Men and women stood in long lines waiting for their dole, as their meagre weekly unemployment pay was called. There were still groups of ex-servicemen, bemedalled veterans from the 1914–18 war, playing band-music in the streets for the pennies of passers-by. Some of these men had wooden legs, sewn-up sleeves, scarred faces. All those unemployed people were known in Scottish parlance as 'the idle', not in any deprecative sense.

There was, in fact, a world depression, counterbalanced by an urge, amongst young people, for change, for a greater freedom of life. This was achievable in everyone's shaky economic circumstances; in fact, with little to lose, the freedom we wanted was all the more realizable. 'Advanced' people, even of our bourgeois acquaintance, began to let their children run naked on the beach. All-vegetable nature-cures became popular. Health and beauty classes sprang up in all parts. 'Do you believe in free love?' intelligent teenagers asked each other. At the same time, there was little sex before marriage among the middle classes. It wasn't unheard of, but mostly it was all talk. Hiking holidays cost hardly anything. Trade competition was evident. Prices everywhere came down and continued sinking till the outbreak of war in 1939.

Before I left school at the age of seventeen I was reading T.E. Lawrence's *The Seven Pillars of Wisdom*, a mighty tome of which I don't remember a word. There was still a moneyed fringe in the country, but money as a factor had been changing hands. Wealth was no longer an attribute of the upper class, and was in fact slowly slipping through the fingers of those who had hung on tight to their fortunes. Many well-known families, at this time, were obliged to treat their own relations as 'paying guests' when they came to stay.

What was I to do with my life? I would have liked to have gone to a university but merely in order to obtain a degree, and that only for the uncertain purpose of getting a better job. I was studious, but I liked my own form of studies, picking and choosing books in the public library. I loved poetry anthologies of all sorts so that I could compare poetic forms and rhythms and consider their aptness for the theme. But I don't know if I would have made a good academic scholar. The chance of finding another inspiring teacher like my later 'Miss Jean Brodie' in the form of Christina Kay was very slight. Anyway, there was really no money for me to go to a university. Even if my fees had been covered by scholarships, the extra expenses involved for over three or four years for a young woman without means, and the meagre chances of getting a job at the end of it, combined to make such an ambition, for me, something of a luxury.

And I saw the reverse side of the situation. I noticed that many older girls who were studying at Edinburgh University in those days were humanly rather dull and earnest, without adult style or charm, indeed there was a puritanical atmosphere. Charm was shunned like a work of the devil. In contrast to the universities of today they were then largely an extension of school. Children matured later than now. I doubt if many of those university students could have told you who Gary Cooper was, Conrad Veidt (my pin-up), Madeleine Carroll, Marlene Dietrich. They could on the other hand write a dissertation on John Donne by the time they were twenty. (But so could I.)

However, I inscribed myself at the Heriot-Watt College (now a university) to complete my education in English prose. I was particularly interested in précis-writing, and took a course in that. I love economical prose, and would always try to find the briefest way to express a meaning. Heriot-Watt College had a reputation for practical and businesslike teaching.

The college, like my school, James Gillespie's, belonged to that group of educational institutions that had been heavily endowed by Edinburgh merchants and benefactors from the sixteenth to the nineteenth centuries. The 'Heriot' of the name referred to that George Heriot (Jingling Geordie), goldsmith and court jeweller. He was commemorated in Sir Walter Scott's *Fortunes of Nigel*. When he died in 1624, his fortune was bequeathed to the founding of a school. The 'Watt' of the college's name was James Watt (1736–1819), most famous for his invention of the steam engine. The watt, a unit of power, is named after him and the term horsepower was first used by him. There is an anecdote often told of James Watt, that his aunt reproved him for indolence: 'I never saw such an idle boy as you; for the last hour you have not spoken one word, but taken the lid off the kettle and put it on again, holding now a cup and now a silver spoon over the steam, watching how it rises from the spout, catching and counting the drops it falls into.'

Heriot-Watt College was subsidized from the Heriot funds, mainly for scientific and technical instruction. The idea of a more scientific atmosphere in general, and a more scientific approach to English, in contrast to the broad, humane, poetry-loving approach of Gillespie's, appealed to me when I started attending classes at the college. My friends thought Heriot-Watt's a strange choice for me. But in fact it offered something I wanted and needed. The use of language in the daily life of commerce, of trade, banking, even politics, was plainly more genuinely based in proportion as it was less rhetorical. I found that the work I put in, and the knowledge I absorbed at Heriot-Watt College was useful – for instance, later in my life when I had a job as an industrialists' speech-writer for a public relations firm. I still find myself fascinated by good managerial-type speech, adopted by the more successful young politicians of the last decade. I find 'managerial' speech unpretentious, direct, quite expressive enough. One doesn't need sermons, figures of speech, drawling cadences and sonorous poetics in modern parliaments, congresses or conventions.

But in order to write about life as I intended to do, I felt I had first to live. From about this time the essentials of literature were, to me, outside of literature; they were elsewhere, out in the world. Life in our part of Edinburgh had changed very little during the 'thirties. A few shops had changed hands. Our upstairs neighbour, good Mrs Kerr, had died, leaving her daughter, the soprano Maudie, still practising her scales and songs every evening. She was presently joined by a handsome baritone a good deal younger than herself who accompanied her in their duets. Maudie gave singing lessons; Bill Logan, the baritone, was, she said, her best pupil. The neighbours were amused to hear his shoes going one-clump, two-clump upstairs on the bedroom floor as he took them off at night. When Maudie and Bill decided to get married, speculation was rife as to whether Maudie would get married in white. In the event, she stopped on the way to her wedding to show us her outfit: autumn tints for herself and her four bridesmaids. They looked extremely theatrical in their large yellow and russet picture hats, and similarly coloured organdie dresses. Although he was the younger, Bill died first, sadly, an alcoholic. Maudie's singing voice, which in fact improved with time, trilled on into the last hours of the night. To go to sleep listening to Maudie insisting on ever higher and higher notes, that she knew that her Redeemer liveth, gave one a sense of continuity.

I loved going to dances with my brother. I was allowed any boyfriends I liked so long as I brought them home. But my favourite men were my brother's much older friends, American medical students. There were three of them to whom my parents took a great affection: Jay Snyder, Dave Simon and Phil Prinz. For many years, in fact until they graduated, they joined us for a special supper every Sunday night, sometimes with other of our friends, so that we had a weekly party at home. Jay was the youngest, the most sensitive, and my mother's favourite. I think he was homesick; he played 'Home Sweet Home' on our piano. One of the others on one occasion introduced a saxophone into the house: 'The music goes round and round . . . and it comes out here.' Now Jay is retired and lives in Florida, and writes to me sweetly about those merry days of our youth.

I was too young as yet to be a girlfriend of any of these students. Both Frances and I had left school the same year, 1935, aged seventeen. When I attended Heriot-Watt College, Frances, I think, went to a secretarial college as did many of my schoolmates who didn't continue on an academic route. Secretarial colleges were expensive, but I knew some secretarial skills would be useful in eventually getting jobs. So I got a teaching job at a small private day school, the Hill School, at 35 Colinton Road in the Merchiston district of Edinburgh not far from my home in Bruntsfield Place. Instead of pay I was given free tuition in shorthand and typing by the school's secretarial teacher. I have found this to be enormously useful all my life. Although I compose by hand it was a great benefit when I first became a published writer to be able to type my own stories and essays quickly. And it is always an advantage for an author to be able to take verbatim shorthand notes of meetings, encounters, chance remarks overheard on a train, in a restaurant.

At the Hill School during the day I taught English, arithmetic and nature studies to small classes, each of about six pupils. There were some small boys and older girls aged from ten to sixteen. Some of the girls, not much younger than myself, were also taking a secretarial course. School work here was not assumed in the serious light I was used to at the school I had attended for twelve years, and just left. The girls were only filling in their school-days until it was time for them to go to a finishing school somewhere on the Continent. The small boys were preparing for boarding schools. Although they were children of wealthy families, they were not over-indulged or spoilt in the slightest way. They were naïve and friendly, somewhat over-sheltered. It was the easiest thing in the world to keep them occupied with this or that lesson. I largely followed their textbooks. Perhaps they learned something from me. What they liked to talk about most were their own brothers, sisters and cousins, naming them, giving their ages, the colour of their hair and eyes.

Even before I had acquired a good standard of shorthand and typing I realized I was being exploited. The Hill School 'for senior girls, and preparatory school for boys' was established in a fairly large house, with a pleasant garden, and was entirely run and owned by two sisters, then in their fifties, the Misses Philip, one fat and one thin, jolly and tart respectively. Again, so very,

very unlike the school I had attended, these headmistresses aimed all their efforts, without pretext, at pleasing the parents. I felt sure that their main thought was to rake in the considerable fees. This is always a danger in privately run schools.

The teacher of shorthand and typing, a faded lady who had no abilities outside of her field, the two sisters and I made up the whole of the staff. It was a genteel and paying concern.

I was giving four or five hours of lessons a day besides helping with casual jobs in the office. For this I was receiving one hour's tuition. After a year I felt it was time that I was paid something. But at that age I wasn't equipped to ask for money, I simply didn't know how to go about it. Instead, I told them that I had to look for a secretarial job, now that I was able to speed along on the typewriter without looking at the keys and slash shorthand across the pages. I thought the sisters were fairly pleased with my teaching so far. I thought then they would ask me to continue and offer me some pay, but no. They just said all right, and let me go. I suppose they soon found another unqualified, unpaid young teacher on the same terms.

For pocket-money, that year, I had at weekends coached a small boy through his repeat year for the vital qualifying examination, which children took at about the age of twelve to move them from the junior to the senior school department. He passed the exam on his second try, and now I was free to look for a job with pay; I was eighteen, and didn't want to depend on my parents any more.

I was adult, although the official coming-of-age was twenty-one. Gone were the days when my father dressed up in a sheet to play the ghost and give me a fright if I came home late. ('Late' was ten o'clock while I was still a schoolgirl.)

The centre of attraction for a job was Princes Street and the stately New Town of lovely squares. On one side of the famous street were the sunken Princes Street Gardens; and, looming above them, the mighty castle rock with the ancient castle on its summit. The other side of the mile-long street was lined with elegant shops and exclusive clubs. I thought it would be good to work near Princes Street, probably in one of the great squares behind it.

Jobs were extremely scarce. I applied for a few which were advertised in the papers, knowing I was one of hundreds. I had a few replies, calling me for an interview. These were very enlightening. Some of the employers, lawyers or town councillors, were curious as to my 'foreign' name, Camberg. (My father had always refused to change his name to 'Camber' as had the rest of the family, his brother and cousins, who were mostly in business. As an employed mechanical engineer my father felt he had nothing to change his name for, and nothing, moreover, to be ashamed of. He used to say, jokingly, that the Royal Family, who had changed their name during World War I from Battenberg to Mountbatten – a literal translation – could do as they liked, but he wasn't going to change to Mountcam.) When asked about my name I said it was a Jewish name, evidently of German origin. This often caused surprise, for I didn't have any particular Jewish features. The Cambergs themselves were fair with blue eyes. In colouring I mainly resembled the Uezzells of Watford. But otherwise I looked rather Scottish with reddish hair, blue eyes and a round face with a sort of bloom. All my youth I was inclined to be fat, sometimes more sometimes less, as the photographs show. I didn't look at all like a poet or an intellectual.

Anti-Semitism was rife in the 'thirties all over Europe, but I can't say that in the Edinburgh of 1936, when I was looking for a job, I had the sense of any racial discrimination. What was difficult was my lack of experience and meagre secretarial qualifications. I was only once 'offended' at one of these interviews, and I have put the word in quotes because actually I was more intrigued than offended. I forget what line of business was concerned. It was a small office with a plump little man no more than thirty. The interview took place after office hours, as was quite normal. I was still eighteen. I was asked to sit on a chair beside his desk. He asked me a few questions, then pulled his chair over to face mine, so that we were almost knee to knee. Then he looked at me with steady piercing eyes without speaking for at least five minutes. I kept my gaze somewhere beyond his shoulder. In the Scotland of those days it was not unusual for employers to 'look well' at candidates for jobs, but I was not so naïve as to suppose that this man was *looking well*. I knew that he was having a good letch, as I called it in my private lingo. My instinct told me not to move. Eventually the interview was at an end. He would write to me, he said, in the usual formula, and let me know his decision. I was amazed when two days later a letter arrived from him asking me politely if I would come for a second interview, to which, of course, I didn't go.

Soon after this I got a job at 106 Princes Street at the west end, in the office of the elderly owner of an exclusive women's department store, William Small & Sons. They took me on without further ado because they liked my letter of application. My sweet employer was William Small himself. His office was really an enormous drawing-room with a grand piano, a luxurious carpet and lots of flowers. My new-found Pitman's shorthand speed was completely wasted on Mr Small's leisurely dictation, punctuated as it was by scraps of meditative philosophy, Scottish wisdom, and sheer information such as 'The majority of old people die in November.' He himself at this time was probably well over seventy. His son, Gordon, a tall, handsome and agreeable young man of thirty who now ran the business, would occasionally come in, play the piano for a while, and go out again. Sometimes I would find Mr Small the elder contemplating a mass of textile samples, cotton in various stripes, from which he was choosing his personal supply of shirts for the forthcoming season. His taste was very avant-garde for an elderly Scot. I helped him to choose the faintly-coloured stripes, then egged him on to agree to ever more bold ones, before compiling a detailed letter ordering the substantial consignment of shirts. Another way in which we passed the dreamy hours was by coping with his considerable list of charities. His system was to donate a sum of money to trustees of a central fund for distribution to the charities which he marked on the list provided by the trustees. With great patient diligence he weighed up the merits and needs of each beneficial fund.

This old-fashioned, tranquil way of using time gave me to wonder how he had built up the flourishing business from which he had retired in favour of his son. In the shop's offices, called the counting house, there was a good deal of industry but no bustle. I went to type letters there, and to help with various jobs when Mr Small stayed at home, which was rarely. (Only the deepest snow-drifts daunted him.) In the middle of the office was a long desk divided length-wise. On each side sat two people, each of whose share of the sloping desk was locked every evening. These four constituted a chief accountant, Miss Ritchie, and three ledger clerks, all women. They bent over their ledgers all day, pen in hand. The pens had fitted nibs or points and they dipped these pens into ink as they worked. Sometimes they dipped into red ink, sometimes into blue. I myself possessed a fountain pen which my brother Philip had given me some years back. But fountain pens were considered rather upstart. These lady-clerks often drew lines with their rulers. I was interested to see how bookkeeping was done, but beyond learning that one ledger was called a Day Book, and the other merely The Ledger, I wasn't encouraged to pry into the firm's secrets.

One of the women-clerks was adept at using a progressive instrument called an adding machine. It was a simple calculator with a keyboard and an immense handle, rather like the cash-registers that were already installed in most shops. Miss Ritchie, though the eldest by at least ten years, well over forty, was by far the most sexy. In fact, she was rather vulgar and told dirty jokes. For that alone, I fairly despised her, and was merely astonished at the abnegation of all femininity in the other three. If they conversed at all at the break for tea (often made by me) they talked about what they had eaten for lunch and how much they had paid for it. (A triumphant record, one day, was three courses for ninepence.) I was much more at home with the three junior assistants of the counting house, teenage girls whom Miss Ritchie bullied or cosseted according to her mood.

My starting pay was three pounds a month. Most young people on my level were paid by the week, but Small's introduced this touch of arch refinement into their system, so that employees could refer to their 'salary' rather than their humble wages. After eight months, however, I was paid six pounds. This doubling of my pay didn't happen at once, but bit by bit in my monthly envelope, so that when I took my pay into the office to show they had made a mistake in my favour, the pay-clerk merely said, 'Thank Mr Small.' I suppose the old gentlman felt I deserved it; certainly I tried to put some originality into his letters. Six pounds a month was enough for a girl to live on fairly well in Edinburgh in 1936, although it would have been difficult to manage on that pay in London. My mother was greatly impressed. I used to treat her to lipsticks and scent (Coty's L'Aimant), besides contributing towards the household expenses. Apart from my pay there were advantages to be drawn from the shop itself, where employees were allowed a discount on any purchases they made. I made as many as I could afford, for I always cared for charming clothes.

Small's was at that time one of the five best women's shops in Edinburgh. The others were Darling's, Jenner's and Forsyth's with Maule's in the running. It was not till later, in the 'seventies, that Small's swallowed Darling's, and later in that decade, totally disappeared.

The shop assistants in these super-elegant establishments all wore long black dresses and walked with a special gliding movement, not unlike the model girls of today. On entering the store, the customer would be greeted by a tall man in morning coat and top hat. He would give a half-bow, a mere inclination:

'Madam desires . . . ?' When Madam had expressed her desire for hosiery, or dresses (all dresses were known as 'gowns'), the tall man, whose designation was 'shop-walker', would gracefully beckon one of the black-gowned sirens: 'Miss Smith, will you attend to Madam?' or 'Miss Fraser, will you conduct Madam to the Outfitting Department?' ('Outfitting' was a euphemism for corsetry, then much in demand. The whalebone variety was giving way to the two-way stretch elastic roll-on. Every woman felt she needed 'support', for some reason.) I was thoroughly intrigued by this perpetual ballet of refinement which started with the first step of a client over the threshold and ended up there in the Dickensian-style counting house where the sales and reckonings were duly entered in the books, and from where accounts were 'rendered'.

My former schoolmate from Gillespie's, Elizabeth Vance, has written to me about those days of the 'thirties when

one could stroll along Princes Street and meet numerous friends quite by chance. . . . And unlike today we knew who owned all the shops — all family businesses at one time — Maules', Jenners', Forsyths' . . . I loved to be taken on a winter's afternoon to Crawfords for 'high tea' — white tablecloths, waitresses in black and white lace-edged aprons, the welcoming lights on and a cheerful fire blazing. Occasionally I would go with my mother to Darling's and if 'Will Y.' was there and greeted us as we entered the store we felt important and our day was made.

Will Y. Darling was not only the owner of Darling's but unlike his rival, Gordon Small, he was his own shop-walker. He could be seen looming inside the entrance to his store, large-built, dressed in his morning coat with striped trousers, his top hat and white gloves, welcoming his customers. 'Willie Darling' was a well-known Edinburgh character, later Sir Will, Lord Provost of Edinburgh.

All the time I was at Small's I never tired of soaking up the mixed atmosphere of luxury, real elegance and silliness. Passing through the glamorous departments on my way to Mr Small's room, I would overhear some of the most affected and absurd scraps of conversation between the clients and the saleswomen that I have ever heard in my life. Airs of condescension on the part of the client and flattery on the side of the saleswomen were rife. I thought often that I would like to write an amusing book called *The Department Store*. I never did, but perhaps I still might. I am sure that my faculties of character-observation were somewhat sharpened by the experience of Small's.

I spent some of my money on gramophone records and books. The records appealed to my father, for we had a radiogram now which we called the grammy. My father's favourite recordings were those of the Italian tenor, Enrico Caruso, who had died in 1921. My mother preferred popular English numbers with a romantic turn which we heard on the late-night radio broadcast by the dance-bands of London hotels. We were all hooked on Charlie Kunz, a dance-music pianist with an original sense of rhythm and beat. He played a number called 'Lazybones'. I don't know who played 'Begin the Beguine' and 'Blue Moon' on the radio; these numbers were played at the dances I went to, once or twice a week. Jazz was moving into swing in the mid- and late 'thirties. There was always someone, mainly a boyfriend, to take me to a film. (I never went alone.) Greta Garbo, then young and prospering, in *Anna Karenina* and *Camille*, and *The 39 Steps* directed by the flourishing Hitchcock, were among those new productions, now oldies, that entered my generation's imagination.

Penguin paperback reprints had started to come out in 1935. They were the first pocket-books in England. The standard price of hardback books was between seven and eight shillings. The first batch of Penguins were sixpence, later ninepence. The public response in those hard-up days of unemployment and low wages was extremely good. I acquired most of the Penguins as soon as they came out. The first was *Ariel* by the French author André Maurois, a good translation of his romance built on the life of Shelley. It is most unreliable as a biography of Shelley, but it has a lot of charm and it was then that I became interested in the lives of nineteenth-century writers, the Shelleys in particular. Sixteen years later I wrote my critical-biography, *Mary Shelley*.

A Farewell to Arms, the next on the Penguin list, introduced me to Ernest Hemingway. My favourite of all in that year of Penguin's launching, 1935, was Eric Linklater's *Poet's Pub*. It was nearest to the world that I felt I was growing up into. In tone, there was a throw-away quality of liberty and humour, so far absent in the modern fiction I was used to; at the same time it was a serious book. Besides, Linklater was a Scot, and I felt a kinship. I still find *Poet's Pub* enjoyable. Agatha Christie was represented in the first batch of Penguin reprints (*The Mysterious Affair at Styles*) and so was Dorothy Sayers (*The Unpleasantness at the Bellona Club*). One immense favourite of the day, *Gone to Earth* by Mary Webb, however, left me quite unaffected and dry-eyed. It was partly in county dialect which I have always abhorred in fiction, even in that of Thomas Hardy. Mary Webb's themes were rustic. Her great popularity was mainly due to the fact that Stanley Baldwin, the pipe-puffing former Prime Minister of Britain, had publicly praised her work.

To reach Small's from my home was a fifteen- to twenty-minute tram-ride. I always returned home for lunch although it was a rush; my mother was now recovered from her previous refusal to be left alone in the house but she got anxious if she didn't set eyes on us all half-way through the day. This meant that I spent well over an hour a day travelling on the tram-car. I spent the time reading the newspaper, mainly *The Scotsman*. Recently, a friend sent me some copies of *The Scotsman* of the late 'thirties from which I can see more precisely than memory could describe, what I read. Very often an article, a reported event or a photograph are perfectly familiar to me. The years 1936 and 1937 come flooding back; I am there on my rattling tram-car, reading about the Spanish Civil War, the latest news to come through on 7 September 1936, the burning of Irun, a town on the French border, by Franco's Insurgents. There is a picture that comes back clearly to me: King Edward VIII (preparations for whose coronation were at their height), sitting with President Kemal Ataturk in an open carriage on a state visit to Turkey – 'King Edward acknowledging the cheers of the crowds . . .' runs the headline. But there are no crowds in the picture, only a few police scattered anxiously on the road. This anomaly I observed at the time; it has been latent in my mind all these years.

The coronation did not come off, and the King's abdication was soon in the air. I heard the King's speech of abdication on the wireless with one of my men-friends, Sydney Oswald Spark, or S.O.S. as we called him, at his club. The next year I became engaged to him.

Among my friends it was a question whether we were pro-Teddy or pro-abdication. My feelings were that it didn't matter one way or another. I didn't see, and still fail to see, what effect it would have on the nation if Wallis Simpson should become his consort. I thought the whole affair amusing and very entertaining and I loved to note the pomposity of the official comments of the time. But since the royal family had no legislative powers I felt, really, that we had the same life, the same opportunities, food and clothes, available to us, whoever sat on the throne.

The government was a different matter. I didn't yet have a vote. It was clear that all political parties in Britain were against Fascism and dictatorships. In 1936 Sir Oswald Mosley, head of the British Fascists, led an anti-Jewish march in one of London's Jewish quarters, Whitechapel. It failed. He had a certain following of a fringe-mob including many thugs, but his movement took no roots at all. Mussolini was a figure of music-hall fun. The menace of Hitler was taken more seriously. At this stage he was considered by a large number of people to be someone who could be reasoned with, who could be 'approached'. But the more intelligent members of society had already perceived the truth. Some refugees from Hitler's persecutions had already settled in Britain with their families, most of them medical doctors and specialists. Hitler's speech on the Nazi Party's tenth anniversary was reported in *The Scotsman*. 'Only posterity', said he, 'would appreciate the full extent of the Nazi achievements.'

I had no specific religion but at the same time I had a strong religious feeling. There were times when, listening to lovely music on the radio, looking at a fine picture in the Scottish National Gallery, reading or writing a poem, I was aware of a definite 'something beyond myself'. This sensation especially took hold of me when I was writing; I was convinced that sometimes I had access to knowledge that I couldn't possibly have gained through normal channels – knowledge of things I hadn't heard of, seen, been taught. I know that such phenomena can possibly be explained rationally in a variety of ways. When I was young, though, the confidence that arose from my sense of receiving 'given' knowledge and ideas constituted my religion. But I never associated this religious mental activity with psychic powers, all claims for which I considered to be entirely phoney. My religious education at school had been Presbyterian for which, with its predominant accent on the lovely Bible, I have always been grateful. Some Jewish observances on my father's side of the family came my way, rather less so than in my brother's education. I always thought with happiness of one Passover night at my Aunt Esther's. Esther, my father's eldest sister, was married to a Turkish Jew, Uncle Isador. This touch of the exotic Orient in my family had been a source of pride to me as a schoolgirl. Uncle Isador pointed out to me on that Passover occasion that the sweet herbs symbolized the joyful interludes of the Jewish passage over the Red Sea, and the bitter herbs symbolized the difficulties. I was inspired by the whole symbolic performance of the ritual feast.

By 1937 some of my friends were getting engaged and married. I longed to leave Edinburgh and see the world. Perhaps that is why I got engaged to Sydney Oswald Spark. I had a diamond ring. S.O.S. was to leave shortly for Southern Rhodesia (now Zimbabwe) for an initial three-year job as a teacher. He was thirteen years my senior. I thought him interesting, as I generally found 'older men'. My parents were not at all keen on the idea of my going so far away at the age of nineteen. They knew very little about S.O. Spark, he had not been working recently in Edinburgh and had few friends there. I had met him at a dance. My father was particularly uneasy. I don't know exactly why I married this man rather than any of the younger boyfriends who took me to dances. I will probably never know. It was a disastrous choice. Unbeknown to us, the poor man had mental problems, not obvious at the time. A friend of mine with whom I discussed this lately has suggested that perhaps he had a hypnotic effect on people. This, strangely enough, was my mother's theory in later years when she had observed his dealings with someone else, and found them inexplicable.

Anyway, I was attracted to a man who brought me bunches of flowers when I had flu. (From my experience of life I believe my personal motto should be 'Beware of men bearing flowers.') I also liked the proposition that I wouldn't have any housework to do 'out there' in Africa, that I would be free to pursue my writing. And, of course, the call of adventure in a strange continent was very strong. My husband-to-be put it to me that he was lonely; I felt sorry for him. S.O. Spark left for Africa before me. After a few months he sent me a one-way ticket to Southern Rhodesia. We were to be married there.

Frances Niven and I had a farewell tea with Miss Christina Kay. Frances, too, was soon to get married. I felt that Miss Kay was looking at me sometimes with a strange sadness. I felt she wished I were not going. I never saw her again. My parents, Philip and an uncle, Joe Shapiro, came to Southampton to see me off on the boat. My father found a friend, a fellow-engineer, on board as a passenger. He was a man of about forty. 'Look after my daughter,' said my father. (That was a laugh; he made every attempt to follow me around making passes, the whole of the two-week voyage.) All passengers' visitors were ordered ashore. It was 13 August 1937, when, alone for the first time in my life, I sailed on the *Windsor Castle* to Cape Town, the first lap on my journey.

Chapter Four

It was in Africa that I learned to cope with life. It was there that I learned to keep in mind – in the front of my mind – the essentials of our human destiny, our responsibilities, and to put in a peripheral place the personal sorrows, frights and horrors that came my way. I knew my troubles to be temporary if I decided so. There was an element of primitive truth and wisdom, in that existence in a great tropical zone of the earth, that gave me strength.

The boat trip from Southampton to Cape Town took fourteen vividly memorable days. I was a third-class passenger, as were most of the young people on the boat. The older ones were part of family groups. There were students or brides-to-be like myself. There were a few valets or lady's maids (whose employers were up in first class). It was an all-white cast of characters.

The younger set had intense fun for two days and nights, dancing to the band and eating quantities of elaborate food at the long tables in the dining-room. I was already dodging the amorous engineer. Then we entered the dreaded Bay of Biscay. In those days few ships had stabilizers to balance them in rough seas; we had none. I knew that the Bay was a terror to cross, and it lived up to its reputation. I rocked and rolled in my bunk, hardly caring whether I lived or died. I staggered up on deck out of curiosity and desire for air. The decks were deserted except for a few sailor hands, who, themselves, looked pretty green in the face. The golden boys and girls of the first nights out were nowhere to be seen. Where had all the flowers gone? I arrived at a bathroom and fetched up everything I had eaten for the whole of my life. In the cabin, my two room-mates were lying feebly supine, having taken some seasickness remedy prescribed by the ship's doctor. The bottle was on the chest of drawers and, urged by my two suffering, weak companions, I poured out a substantial swig of the near-lethal draught. I suppose I swallowed it, for I woke up thickly a day later, when we were clear of the Bay of Biscay and life on the *Windor Castle* had begun to resume its cheerful noise.

Most of the memorable experiences of my life I have celebrated, or used for a background in a short story or novel. It strikes me only now to wonder why I have never written about life on board a passenger ship. Perhaps one day I will do so, it's a good idea. I can think of no better setting for a story or a novel than that fourteen-day trip between Southampton and Cape Town, with our mixed and bohemian crowd. Numerous privileged young first- and second-class passengers used to slink down daily to join us in third where the action was.

I remembered, years later, that doctor's overloaded brew during a crossing of the Atlantic in the early 'sixties on the *Queen Mary*. I was with my editor, Alan Maclean. We both felt queasy. It was a very rough crossing. (But nothing like the one on the Bay of Biscay so many years before or even a nasty heave-around I experienced on a wartime troop-ship zigzagging from the Cape to Liverpool via the Azores.) This crossing on the *Queen Mary*, comparatively mild as it was, sent us to the ship's nurse. She arrived in our cabins with one of those old-fashioned non-disposable syringes loaded with something strong. We were both laid out for three days, the best part of the trip. When we finally saw each other again, about the last day out, we concluded without hesitation that these maxi-doses were handed out to anyone who complained, to keep them quiet, as is reputedly the case in prison. Al and I decided that never again would we complain at sea.

But back to 1937 and the lively boat of the Union Castle Line. I had heard of shipboard romances and I didn't see why I shouldn't have a mild flirtation, especially as I was to settle down in marriage so soon. And I had a very good reason to find a young man who was fun to dance with and play deck games with; it helped to throw off the attentions of that snooping engineer (he was rather sullen all the voyage). But my boyfriend was a good-looking very fair South African student of twenty travelling home with his parents. He took me more seriously than I intended, and even his parents took the most unusual step of asking me if I was quite sure I wanted to proceed to Rhodesia. I sat with them, all three, and showed them my hand with my diamond engagement ring. It was really rather touching that they wanted me so much to stop off at Cape Town and marry their son. Did they sense that I was making a mistake in my proposed marriage? I often wondered later on. Certainly I encouraged the young man more than I had meant. Anyhow, we had a lot of fun on that voyage. We sat out on deck under the Milky Way, we danced to the band, we listened to the many concerts given by the two fellow-passengers who happened to be professional musicians – he a cellist, she a singer – and who had discovered each other quite by chance, stretched in our deck chairs in the sun until it got too hot for our tender skins.

The boat stopped at Madeira. Down the precarious rope ladder we climbed, into a waiting rowing boat, which took us to the island. Madeira was truly an island of dreams in the days before the tourist boom. Flowers proliferated – mainly dahlias, bright-coloured daisies, carnations, anemones. The Madeirans pressed garlands on us, and bouquets of flowers. I saw, for the first time, the rich cultivation of guavas, mangoes, bananas, papaws, oranges. The women had a special way of embroidering white linen tea cloths with coffee-brown thread. (This embroidery had been introduced to the island in 1850 by an English-woman.) Some of the designs were magnificent. I bought a modest tea cloth for less than five shillings and that was the only item in my 'trousseau'. My husband was not trousseau-minded and neither was I. To people like us, the gifts of the intellect were considered enough. But my Madeira tea cloth reminded me for many years of my day on the beautiful island, where the flowers and fruit luxuriated, where the cathedral held only a few worshipping peasant women with dark-grey shawls.

South we went along the coast of Africa, crossing the tropic of Cancer, crossing the Equator (with a great deal of ducking ceremony around the swimming pool), and passing into the tropic of Capricorn. I was amazed to see the legendary Southern Cross hanging in the sky, in bright reality. The waters at night glittered with phosphorus. All day, the flying fish leapt like ballet dancers. I felt like a real adventurer of the globe.

My South African friends made me promise to write often and come to see them soon. When the boat reached Cape Town we said only a temporary goodbye. It was very strange. For some reason that family of three, the father, the mother and the boy student, were convinced that I wouldn't stay long in Rhodesia. They gave me their address: 'always a home to come to'. In fact I never saw them again. My shipboard boyfriend wrote to me in Rhodesia about a year later. He sent the photographs they had taken on board and in Madeira. I didn't reply. I was already facing problems.

At Cape Town, as I was a minor, Thomas Cook, the travel agents, had an official waiting for me with 'Thomas Cook' printed prominently round the band of his peaked cap. He was to deliver me to the guard on the train to Salisbury (now Harare), capital of the then Southern Rhodesia. Behold, he had a brown-coloured young attendant with him, bearing a bunch of flowers for me! I was taken right back to my school-days: Miss Christina

Kay describing to the spellbound class her thrilling experiences in Egypt and the dragoman coming to say goodbye, bearing a bunch of flowers for her; I remembered my mother's comment, 'Thomas Cook paid for those flowers.' (In my case it had been my future husband – bearer of flowers – who had ordered them.) On the train to Salisbury, the flowers were placed on my table in the dining-room. I felt very much a woman of the world.

Southern Rhodesia was a self-governing colony, which meant that it had its own parliament and also a Governor representing the British monarch. The country came under the vague shadow of the Dominions Office, allied to the Colonial Office, especially in the field of Native Affairs. But the parliament, consisting of elected members, all white, ran the internal business of the country. The law, like that of most of colonial Africa, was Roman Dutch. It was an unusual situation, never very satisfactory. The number of whites in 1937 was about fifty-five thousand. The blacks numbered about one and a half million, rapidly increasing.

I don't know how anyone could have thought of this situation as anything but temporary. To me at the time, there was no feeling of permanence, and I marvelled at people newly arrived from England, who had every intention of remaining for ever. They thought the country was an extension of South Africa. But the spirit of the times in those years between the two world wars was already decidedly against the South African model. Southern Rhodesia was then fifty years old and the pioneering spirit pervaded the atmosphere. I didn't and couldn't pretend to belong. I intended to stay for the pre-arranged three years and gain as much human experience as I could.

Because most of Zimbabwe is on a plateau four or five thousand feet above sea-level, the climate is sub-tropical. I arrived in the spring, just before the beginning of the rainy season and the hottest months. I was married in Salisbury, in the magistrate's office, on 3 September 1937, but not before there had been a technical hitch.

I was a minor of nineteen. Where, demanded the magistrate, a Mr Smith, was my father? Without his permission I could not get married. It had never occurred to me to bring a letter of permission from my father. Cables were sent off to my parents and also to the High Sheriff of Edinburgh; only his word, on the strength of my father's affidavit, would satisfy the Rhodesian authorities. My father, in Edinburgh, swore his assent – reluctantly, as I knew, and as he later confirmed. Finally the permission reached Rhodesia and the marriage took place.

Soon I was settled in rooms in the hotel at Fort Victoria, where my husband's job was. Fort Victoria, a small town in the southern part of the country, was close by the famous Zimbabwe Ruins, and in those comparatively early days the ruins were still surrounded by thick jungle bush and vegetation. The approach was a narrow clearing. I am still glad that I got my first sight of this wonderful complex of Bantu antiquity more or less as it must have been when it was first 'discovered' by the intrepid explorers of the nineteenth century. The ruins are now said to date from about the ninth century and to be the product of a local African folk who lived and worshipped there. The remains consist of a stone-wall maze covering the floor of a valley. The walls are high, about eight feet; at one point they surround a cone-shaped tower about thirty feet high. A short distance away, a hill of granite stones and boulders leads up to what is known as the 'acropolis' – layers of enclosures, which are thought to have been dwelling places – and to a distinctive building that fulfilled a religious function. Frieze carvings along the walls led many early archaeologists to speculate that the ruins were the original King Solomon's Mines, of Abyssinian or Phoenician origin. But whether or not this evidence of the Zimbabwe civilization, rising as it does out of the harsh, uncultivated jungle, was the original inspiration of Rider Haggard's novel, the evidence of radio-carbon and other more recent tests appears to prove that the ruins are indeed of indigenous African origin.

During my first weeks in Rhodesia I loved to go there. Life in Fort Victoria was too lazy and slow for me. It was simply an adaptation of English village life, of which I knew little at first hand. The wife of the chemist, the doctor, the Church of England vicar, the wives of the other schoolmasters all called on me, leaving two cards (or maybe three), one with the corner turned down. I had no calling cards and didn't intend to have any. Actually, I felt too young and too intelligent for all that formal married-woman business. Almost immediately, I was looking forward to getting home again in three years' time, and for that reason I was determined to absorb all I could of these exotic surroundings. The flowers were exceedingly quick-flowering and bright, especially the convolvulus, which sprinkled the veldt half an hour after the rain. The first colours of spring were yellow, brown, gold. Later they turned to green.

It struck me right away what good-looking people the blacks of that area were. It was rightly said that education could give whites an intellectual advantage over blacks, but what was never mentioned, never breathed, was that in spite of a poor diet, spartan shelter, and inadequate medicine the African natives of Southern Rhodesia were, as physical examples of the human race, vastly superior to the average white men and women around them. A great many of the Rhodesian blacks were magnificent. Compared with them, the conquering race looked as if it had only just emerged milk-fed from some nursery. The European women were wrinkled early, parched with the sun.

I had nobody to talk to. Some miles away – but too many miles, as I know now – lived Doris Lessing, then a young girl like me, still in her teens. How I would have loved to have someone like Doris to talk to. She was a Rhodesian by upbringing, and I am sure she already had a distinguished mind. But I didn't meet Doris till many years later.

The white women mainly went around clutching a hundred-cigarette box of Gold Leaf cigarettes (the Rhodesian brand) in their hands, with a lighted cigarette perpetually drooping out of the side of their mouths. I didn't like these women. When we next moved, to Salisbury, they proliferated. They were very sure of themselves as women. In the colony, there was one white woman to three white men, which led to violent situations – sometimes to murder – among the men.

Some women of my acquaintance wore a key on a cord around their necks. This key was to lock up the sugar against the black servants. 'They steal as much as a pound at a time,' said one of the women to me. I ventured that maybe the servants needed the sugar. This observation was regarded as blasphemy. Indeed, there was no way in which one could really befriend a native African, for dire penalty wrought by Heaven and earth for such a course of action fell not in the least on the white befriender but on the black befriended. I think if I had sat down in the kitchen to have my morning coffee with my cook, Moses, nobody would have said a word to me. But Moses would have been made to feel 'his place' in a hundred different, petty ways.

All the same, by the time I reached Rhodesia, various reforms had been introduced (always by pressure from London, against the wishes of the Rhodesian whites). In my day, no black African stepped off the pavements to make way for a passing white, as had been required previously by law. Young, homeless blacks who did not want to work on the land were not beaten into submission but were left alone, thanks to a public outcry in England. But sometimes I was horrified by the stories I was told, mainly by Afrikaners, or people of South African Dutch origin – who would proudly narrate this or that story of how an impertinent black had been 'fixed'. My story 'The Curtain Blown by the Breeze' contains such an incident: a farmer, I was told, on returning home found a piccanin (as we called a small black boy) standing outside the windows of his wife's room, peeping at her through the curtains while she breast-fed the baby. For this crime, he shot the piccanin dead. This story was told me by a smug, self-satisfied South African Dutch woman of about forty-five, whom I met in one of the many boarding-houses I lived in during my married life. (My husband was quarrelsome; we were always being posted elsewhere.) The woman seemed to think the farmer was quite right and to regret that things were changing or had changed. I was unable to speak. I simply stared at the woman. She didn't notice this, but went on talking in her self-righteous way. The farmer, she lamented, went to prison for three years.

I remember a similar woman (and she was typical of many men) sitting at our table one mealtime, describing how a man of her acquaintance, driving along one of the Rhodesian highways (which were tarmac only in strips), deliberately knocked dead a black cyclist who refused to get off one of the strips to accommodate the car coming behind him. 'That fixed him, that fixed him,' said the woman, heaving her prominent bosom with the utmost satisfaction. Again, I was struck silent, as was my husband. Our friends of British origin were much more reasonable and civilized in their attitude, but the rough, frontier-type atmosphere was often unpleasant; it entered one's soul. I knew I could never make my home in such conditions.

When I was expecting a baby, my husband suggested, very earnestly, that I have an abortion. He was beginning to feel uneasy and unstable. I refused. My son, Robin, was born in Bulawayo on 9 July 1938, at the Lady Rodney Nursing Home, after a labour of a day and a half – far too long. I was at the end of my strength and didn't expect that either I or my baby would survive, and, indeed, it was a miracle that we both emerged strong and healthy. I had bitten down one of my nails. My husband brought me a manicure set and a bunch of flowers. He began to show signs of the severe nervous disorder from which he had suffered and was to suffer all his life. He had fits of violence, and continued to quarrel with everybody. I now had news from my parents, in Edinburgh, that his sister had been committed as an insane person. In a lucid moment, my husband said, 'One day this will all appear to you as a bad dream.' I knew he was right. Plainly, he needed professional help. We had no marital life after the birth of my son. I made one trip with my husband to the Victoria Falls, hoping this would make him feel better. That by itself was wonderful; but I knew my married life was over. Strangely, the experience of the Victoria Falls gave me courage to endure the difficult years to come. The falls became to me a symbol of spiritual strength. I had no settled religion, but I recognized the experience of the falls as spiritual in kind. They are one of those works of nature that cannot be distinguished from a sublime work of art.

I think everyone should try once to visit this true wonder of the world; it should become a sort of Mecca and place of pilgrimage for the human race. I don't know why peace conferences are not held in the vicinity of the Victoria Falls. I can think of no other experience that makes for the reasonable contemplation of our humanity, and a sense of the proportions in which we should think.

Some years later when I was working on my own as a free-lance writer in London I wrote a short story 'The Seraph and the Zambesi' specially for a story competition that had been announced in *The Observer*. In that story (which, happily for me, won the prize) I felt a compulsion to describe the Zambesi River and the approach to the falls through the mysterious Rain Forest as a mystical experience. I expressed, symbolically, how the aridity of the white people there had affected me.

The falls occur in the middle of the course of the wide Zambesi River, where it borders Zambia (formerly Northern Rhodesia) to the north, and Zimbabwe, to the south. The precipice that forms the waterfall is three hundred and fifty-five feet at its deepest. The waters drop into a churning chasm formed by the opposite wall of the precipice, and it is there one stands to watch the grandeur of the scene which no statistical measurement of widths, heights and depths can adequately convey. The usual route to the falls leads through a heavily wooded area known as the Rain Forest, since it is filled with the spray. I remember that on my way through this forest I saw a man covered with oilskins (as I was) for protection from the spray; this man looked about twelve feet tall, and the trees were equally magnified by some peculiarity of the incessant and beautiful vapour. At a distance of about two hundred feet, you begin to hear the tumult of the falls. Then it becomes a roar. *Musioa-tunya* – the smoke that thunders – is the name given to the falls by the local tribes. Amid this great roar, one looks up, one looks down, and from side to side: no more sky, no more forest – everywhere is a mighty cascade of water.

The Zambesi River itself was another unforgettable marvel. I went on a steamboat among rhinoceroses and crocodiles, with low trees lining the shore crowded with chattering monkeys and alive with happy and agile small boys making fun among the voracious-looking orchids.

My days in Salisbury and Bulawayo were nothing like as happy as the times I spent in the country. I loved to visit the farms. There was a more relaxed, democratic atmosphere on the land, where whites and blacks could work together unceremoniously.

In Bulawayo I contracted septicaemia and nearly died. I remember only a screen round my bed and faces peering at me. Dr Rose Sugarman, who later became a close friend, said, 'You're very ill.' I said, 'I know.' Two days later, I sat up in bed and ate the best part of a box of chocolates that someone had brought me. There were still no antibiotics in those days. The cure was aspirins and, I suppose, youth.

I wrote home a nostalgic letter, pining for those games of golf that I used to enjoy in Edinburgh, even though sporadically. There were golf courses in both Salisbury and Bulawayo. My father sent me a handsome set of clubs in a smart golf bag. He had already bought me a small diamond watch to celebrate the birth of my son; he kept it for me, not wishing to trust the mail. I have the watch to this day but not the clubs, and I wonder what happened to them in all the vicissitudes of my life in Africa.

We were transferred from place to place. This was a drawback from the domestic aspect, and it certainly reflected an uneasiness in my husband's career. But drawbacks can be advantages if you think in the opposite direction. This unsettled life gave me, at least, a full knowledge of the country. The place I enjoyed living in most was one that few people envied. It was Gwelo, a farming area in the central part. Gwelo was still primitive. I felt I was living in the real Rhodesia of the pioneers. We had no electricity, and instead used paraffin lamps, which needed constant attention. Water was carried for miles in petrol cans on the shoulders of our housemen every morning. We managed a weekly bath. The rainy season brought thudding rain and sudden storms followed by a hot calm, in which flying ants would wriggle out of cracks in the wall. My little son was immensely happy in Gwelo. The blacks there were amiable and extremely kind, especially to toddlers. My son was difficult to feed, but I would often find him down in the native quarters eating with them round the mealie pot.

By the time I had been in Africa two years, I thought of leaving my husband. He became a borderline case, and I didn't like what I found either side of the border. He got more and more violent. I thought I could argue rationally with him. This never worked for any length of time. When Nita McEwen, a friend from school, was killed that night by her husband in the hotel where I was staying, I got seriously frightened. My husband had a small revolver, a 'baby Browning', which he liked to fire off in corridors and courtyards. I hid it, and refused to hand it over when he demanded it.

It was exactly two years after my marriage that war broke out. This put an end to my plans to leave the country. No civilians were allowed to leave Rhodesia. Transport, except for intercity trains, was put exclusively at the disposal of the military. After 3 September 1939, no passenger shipping was normally available.

My husband joined the Army. He moved to the Air Force and back again to the Army. I took on a responsible nanny, a 'coloured' (mixed-blood) girl called Esther, and together we moved to new lodgings with my child. I had now officially left my husband. Stuck in Africa, I had to get jobs, but Esther was extremely reliable and affectionate towards me and my son. Her father had been a white magistrate from Durban, her mother a Zulu.

I started the long, weary process, as it then was, of divorce. It was especially difficult under the Roman Dutch law which prevailed in the colony. Even in Britain, at that time, the last thing that could be revealed was 'collusion', or agreement between the parties. If collusion was suspected by the judge, the divorce was endlessly held up, and if it was proved, the divorce fell through. When there were offspring, the law favoured the man. The very mention of mental instability or cruelty in either of the partners was enough to ruin the case; these factors were grounds for legal separation, but not for divorce. The grounds for divorce were infidelity (especially on the woman's part) and desertion. I chose desertion. My husband would not desert me, so I deserted him. I made a private agreement to pay for the divorce, which my father most willingly did, digging into his hard-won savings to meet the legal fees. He also augmented my income and eventually paid for my voyage home. It was good fortune that in his last years I enjoyed sufficient literary success to be able to make his life more comfortable, in turn. The good fortune was really mine: nothing can repay goodness, love, and loyalty.

My father had never liked S.O.S., but now he thoroughly despised him. My mother, with more understanding, was sorry for him, and later on, when he returned to Edinburgh for an endless series of cures, she did her best to make him feel he had a friend. Small thanks she got.

I, too, was sorry for the man I had married. But I was reminded of a recent novel by Stefan Zweig entitled *Beware of*

Pity that treats of a young officer who is induced by pity to get engaged to a crippled girl. Finally he cannot keep up the pretence. The girl, aware of having been misled, commits suicide. Though the material circumstances of the story were far from mine, the elements of pity and compassion were always present. If my husband had not been an object of pity, I would have been much tougher.

For a young woman my life was extremely difficult. One night, having been asked to a dance by a party of friends, I was dancing innocently with a Dr Shankman, who was an eye specialist whom I knew. My husband appeared and set up a fight with him on the dance-floor. My husband was removed, of course, and the doctor and I went on dancing, but this sort of harassment made me hesitate to go around with my friends. It isolated me considerably.

As it was, I escaped for dear life. If I had not insisted on a divorce, God knows what would have happened. I told the man as frankly as I could that I had no intention of living with him again but that if he agreed to a divorce I might possibly be able to help him. I was faithful to my word, but, as it turned out, the possibility of helping him in any dedicated way was plainly beyond me. 'You were the capable one. You were the strong one,' he wrote in his letters from a mental hospital after the divorce. The letters are full of self-recrimination and self-blame but, as a friend wrote and confirmed to me at the time, 'self' was obviously the operative idea. 'You tell me to "snap out of it" but I'm damned if I can,' he wrote to me in October 1944, after I had left Africa. I realized that some people simply cannot help themselves by thinking of others; it is perhaps unkind to expect it.

After my divorce I retained my husband's name, to be the same as my son. This was generally the custom unless one married again. I was glad of this later when I began my literary career. Camberg was a good name, but comparatively flat. Spark seemed to have some ingredient of life and of fun.

I wanted to start my life afresh, and, as well as I could, I did so. Not long after my husband went into the Army, I had my son's eyes tested at Dr Shankman's, and met his receptionist, a young, very pretty, and natural woman, May Heygate. She had a small girl, Gail, about the same age as Robin. May's husband, Nick, was now in the Army and she, like me, was making do in furnished rooms. We liked each other instantly. May suggested we share a flat. Although May had settled for a job as a receptionist to give her more time with Gail, she was a brilliant classics scholar, from Bristol University. I had found a secretarial job with a glamorous businessman, Basil Frost, who had a trading establishment in Bulawayo.

May and I moved in together with our furniture and our two nannies. We were looked after by Moses, the ever-faithful cook. Moses was reserved and dignified. 'One of Nature's gentlemen,' said May. Besides being kindly by nature, he was a mission-educated man. The much-maligned missionaries were in fact the finest people in the colony. Africans flourished and were well educated in their care. Zimbabwe owes its independence in part to the influence of the Christian missions. One of the most saintly men in the colony was an Anglican missionary and poet, Arthur Shearley Cripps, who frequently went cold or hungry because he had given the coat off his back or his dinner to an African. Strangely enough, he was deeply respected by the whites.

May and I shared our flat in Bulawayo for some years. In the mean time the first part of my divorce proceedings was completed. This was the decree nisi, which preceded the decree absolute, due in about a year's time. My husband was already in the nervous-disorders hospital. May's husband, charming Nick, fell ill and died of pneumonia. May and I stood together under a great many vicissitudes. She was so very pretty, a natural ash-blonde, that a great many men wanted to woo her. For my part, the charming Basil Frost (twenty years my senior) spent a lot of time gazing at me over the desk, telling me how young and fresh I was, and explaining how these facts affected him. The truth was that neither May nor I was ready for love affairs; there was a cloud of sadness over both our lives. We felt a predominant concern for our toddlers, and very isolated from home. We would take the children for picnics at weekends, and to the cinema (called the 'bioscope') to see Lassie, who was already a star. Davy Crockett was also a great hero with both children. Popeye was not thought much of.

I thought I might get a job as a junior teacher and applied for a job at an Anglican convent school. I thought it would be convenient to have an infant school for Robin at the place where I worked. I had four interviews in all. A friend of mine who taught at the school told me, after my first interview with the Mother Superior, that I had made a great impression, 'so young and fresh.' These words rang a bell all right: Basil Frost, the ardent heart-throb. And my friend added, 'She loves your complexion and your golden hair.'

What about my abilities? In my second interview, the Mother Superior told me that there might be an opening at the school for me. 'You see,' she said, 'the trouble with this war is the Jews. We need more people like you.' She went on for some time in this vein, sometimes gazing at me in a most wonder-struck way. This woman, fairly well put together physically, somewhere in her forties, was thoroughly obsessed by the Jews; a hatred came through her teeth that I had never experienced before. I murmured that Hitler's propaganda was . . . She wouldn't let me finish. Hitler's quite right, she said. The war is all the fault of the Jews.

At home, I said to May that I was going back again to the convent to see how far the Mother Superior would go. May thought this a lark. But before the fourth interview, which was to be the decisive one for my employment, I told May, 'Today's the day. I'll tell her I'm a Jew.'

This I did. I didn't say part-Jew or any other sort of Jew. I just said, 'Of course, I'm a Jew.'

She said, 'It's not so.'
I said, 'What isn't so?'
She said, 'What you *just said.*'

I took my fair skin and my golden locks right out of there. At the gate I found May waiting for me with our two infants crammed into one push-cart. We bought ice creams all round and sauntered home.

All this time I had never stopped writing poetry. I entered twice for the Rhodesian annual poetry competition and won twice. I published in local magazines. One of the poems was called 'The Go-Away Bird', about the haunting cry of the grey-crested lourie that one could hear all over the veldt of the colony. The bird cried 'go-'way, go-'way'. I felt that it spoke to me, and in later years, my long short story 'The Go-Away Bird' expressed the intermittent sad feelings of those years, the ignorant ill-will of some of the Boer farmers, and the disillusionment of some who had longed for 'home', in an England they had never known, and who found there everything cold, changed, and many people on the make. I was really, myself, a 'Go-away Bird'.

While on the subject of the effect of my African experience on my subsequent work, I should mention my radio-play *The Dry River Bed*, based on a real episode in my life in Africa when a car I was driving got into a rut and went into a dry river bed, smashing the car. Another story, 'The Portobello Road', touches on the then Southern Rhodesia and the great difficulties of mixed marriages there.

In 1942, at the beginning of my period of comparative freedom, and while waiting for the finalization of my divorce, I went to parties and dances occasionally, quite rightly urged by my friends. The Air Force had mounted an immense air-training scheme, and one was always meeting cheery young men just out from home. One of these was a young flight lieutenant who had been through the Blitz, Arthur Foggo. I had a soft spot for Arthur, and that was all; at the same time, it was a lot. His sentiments went much further. We really had a charming time together. Then Arthur was posted home with his group. Overcome by sadness once more, I saw him off at the station to Cape Town from where they would sail for England. Two days later, on 6 October 1942, came a wire from Cape Town. It read: 'Leaving immediately will write you as soon as I arrive. Love Arthur Foggo.' I was rather surprised, knowing the secretive rules of those wartime days, that Arthur's wire had beat the censor. It was extraordinarily specific. It was handed in at 6.17 p.m. and arrived in my hands after ten that night.

South Africa was officially an ally in the war, but an insipid and reluctant one, as I found when presently I spent some time in Cape Town waiting for a boat home. I have often wondered how many of Arthur's friends sent messages that evening so openly revealing their movements. Whether they were betrayed by spies or were simply victims of chance, there was a torpedo waiting in the seas outside Cape Town for their ship. Arthur and his companions went down with it that night. It was about two weeks later that I heard the news. Some of the airmen had left behind them girls whom they had recently married. The men had been extremely popular. The whole colony was in mourning.

May was trying to wangle a passage home. Our friends wrote to describe the horrors of wartime England. But I was now determined to see wartime England. I wanted to be involved. Life in the colony was eating my heart away, and in my depression at Arthur Foggo's death I felt I didn't care what bombs would fall about my ears.

By the end of 1943, it was expected that the war would be over in a few months. There was a possibility of getting on a boat to England if one could reach Cape Town. There was no question of transporting children to England at that stage of the war. I decided for my sanity's sake to go ahead by myself. I had met some very good Catholic nuns at the Dominican convent school in Gwelo. Quite a few young children separated from their parents by the war were at boarding school there. I was satisfied that Robin would be safe in that convent school, and so he was. Even my husband in the mental home, asserting on paper his legal 'rights', liked the nuns of Gwelo. Robin was able to play with the children of my friends there. They also kept an eye on him. A friendly professional childminder and her family had Robin home almost every day, and supported me greatly with constant letters. When I left Rhodesia, Esther, who had been in another job for some time, unexpectedly turned up at the station to see me off. We were sad to leave each other.

My plan was to prepare for Robin to go and live with my parents, who were pining to have him as soon as the war was over and the transport ban lifted. This worked remarkably well. I arrived in England in March 1944. My little son joined me in September of the following year and was greeted with great joy by both my parents. So far as my mother was concerned, her grandson made a remarkable difference to her life. She had been going through a period of depression, probably menopausal. Earlier in the war my parents had taken in a little refugee German girl in response to the Save the Children movement. She had now gone to her relatives in the United States, but my parents were missing her a lot. But now, when Robin arrived, my mother felt thoroughly rejuvenated and Robin took to her from the start. It was a great good thing, and an immense relief to me that he finally had a settled home with my mother and father in Edinburgh. My father was really a second father to my son.

My escape from Southern Rhodesia had been effected by a ruse. I obtained a magistrate's permit (from the same magistrate, Mr Smith, who had officiated at my marriage) to visit Cape Town for three months in order to study literature and drama. I simply didn't go back. I put my name down for a passage to England with a shipping line. I took some jobs while waiting, but

I was very impoverished at this stage. Jobs were ill-paid, especially for English girls who were looked down on by the Afrikaners. Afrikaans policemen would not answer if you asked the way in English. Jobs were also scarce. There were strikes, and an air of economic depression. My life for the few months I was there waiting for transport was enlivened by Marie Bonaparte (Princess Marie of Greece), with whom I struck up a friendship on the basis of our literary interests. She lived with the rest of the Greek royal family in exile, in a fairly small villa. That house was to me an oasis of civilization.

The then Princess (later Queen) Frederica of Greece, whom I was to meet again many years later, in exile in Rome, occupied the upper floors with her rowdy small son (now ex-King Constantine). Marie Bonaparte had bright, dyed red hair, and shrewd eyes sunken into an elderly face. It was simply astonishing to hear her talk so seriously and with such a powerful intelligence, completely regardless of the trappings of exile around her.

Her bedroom, where often we had to sit when the drawing-room was engaged, had the air of what I had come to associate with the few Russian exiles I had come across or heard of, or the Jewish professors and their wives, who had taken refuge in Southern Rhodesia. The mantelpiece of Marie Bonaparte's room was crowded with family photographs in silver frames, a large package of Bemax (a bedtime beverage), some tattered papers, a book of poems by Edgar Allen Poe, on whom she was writing a book, and a pretty vase.

We discussed literature, which she, having been a prominent pupil of Sigmund Freud, approached from a psychological point of view – something quite new to me. I was intrigued, but I felt it left too much unsaid. I had an idea that there was such a thing as a 'literary sense', with which some readers or critics were endowed in addition to the normal five senses, and that it was by this 'sense' that one should judge literature.

Princess Marie's drawing-room was more elegant and

impersonal than the bedroom-study. A (white) butler took one's gloves and brought in the tea. I cannot recall very much of our actual conversation, but I remember that I found Marie Bonaparte's company enormously interesting. She seemed equally eager to hear what I had to say, although this must have been very little. But I let her see my poems, and I think she was sincere in her admiration.

My reading over the past years had been very limited, though intense. In Rhodesia I had little to choose between popular novels, which I hated, or Shakespeare and the Bible, which I read assiduously. Sometimes, by some fortune, I would find a copy of Penguin New Writing, which I fell upon voraciously. I read Eliot. I read what I could find of Ivy Compton-Burnett.

Cape Town was much more civically evolved, but it was still rather empty of intellectual life. I think Marie Bonaparte felt this, too. She was quite indifferent to politics. The encroachment of Communism, which everyone predicted with horror in those days, did not dismay her. In one of her letters to me after I had returned to England she wrote, 'The Russians are a very artistic people. Art will not die therefore.'

When I went to say goodbye to Marie Bonaparte she gave me a letter to carry to Anna Freud in London. I took it to Miss Freud, who pressed me for news of her friend – how she was keeping and how I thought she was managing. I was puzzled then, and still am, that Anna Freud could not get this information through the ordinary mail. Surely the two friends corresponded? But perhaps there were things, in those days of wartime censorship, which could not be written between a member of the Greek royal family and the daughter of Sigmund Freud. Indeed, I had been rather surprised that the letter I carried was in a gummed-down envelope. That was certainly unusual.

There had been an atmosphere of unreality about Cape Town. The community was divided into three: coloured, black and white. The coloured comprised Malays, Indians and people of mixed blood. There were three entrances to the cinemas, and other public places, labelled 'Coloured', 'Black' and 'White'. I thought this quite amusing when I didn't think it tragic. The buses bore the warning 'Do Not Spit' in English and Afrikaans. I had a room in a district called The Gardens where certain visiting naval officers of all nationalities would arrive at odd hours to visit Girlie Lonsdale, an ageing gentleman who occupied the room opposite. My story 'The Pawnbroker's Wife' is set in Cape Town. I think it expresses what to my mind was a refusal of the white people of South Africa to face the human facts around them. They were in 'a world of their own'. Their very speech was surrealistic. Even more than in Rhodesia I felt that their world was not the real world. I wanted the reality of home, even though it meant the bombs of war.

In late February 1944, I was told that there was a passage for me on a troop-ship. This merely meant that some space normally intended for troops returning to England had not been fully occupied. Just like the troops, the thirty or so women who had decided to risk such a voyage were packed into a section with four-tiered bunks. We were told not to undress for bed but to sleep in our dark trousers. Dark trousers, said the typewritten instructions, were advisable should the boat be torpedoed, because sharks tended to overlook dark clothes. (I am sure this was a mess-room jollification.) At all hours we had to hug our lifebelts. We were allowed to wash in salt water. In fact, we were treated no worse and no better than the Army.

The boat, which was bound for Liverpool, did not go there direct. Always forestalling the German U-boats, it zigzagged. We went from Cape Town to Liverpool by way of the Azores. The voyage took three weeks. Before leaving Cape Town I had bought some poetry books. It was ages since I had read new poetry. In pamphlet form I had found T.S. Eliot's *The Dry Salvages* which I read on that dangerous journey.

It was indeed a dangerous journey. But it is curious how a sense of danger diminishes in proportion to the number of people who participate in the risk. On this, as on other occasions during the war, being 'in it together' took the edge off fear. I had no regrets about leaving Africa, and was only too happy to arrive in Liverpool, grim and unheated as it was, on a blacked-out night in March.

CHAPTER FIVE

All women who were under forty-five and who were free of family ties (such as young children or ailing relatives) were under obligation to register for work in wartime England. All types of work were considered to be war service.

In the spring of 1944 after I had been reunited with my family in Edinburgh on my return from Africa, I went to London to find a job which, in any case, I needed. Believe it or not, I chose London rather than peaceful Edinburgh because I wanted to 'experience' the war. This, my incredible ambition, was amply fulfilled on my first night in the blacked-out city. The train got in after dark and I put up at the Euston Station hotel. It was not long before the sirens wailed. I had so far only heard them on the newsreels. The fire-wardens were shouting from the streets to anyone who was not observing the black-out from the darkened windows. This was a period of intense incendiary bombing. It went on all night. Many people in the hotel congregated in the basement regions, but I decided to take my chance in my room. Most people agreed that you took a chance wherever you were.

But soon I was established at 82 Lancaster Gate, the Helena Club, which had been founded long since by a daughter of Queen Victoria, the worthy Princess Helena, for 'Ladies from Good Families of Modest Means who are Obliged to Pursue an Occupation in London'. This was the original 'May of Teck Club' in my novel *The Girls of Slender Means*.

The Helena Club was absolutely charming. It was my home in London from time to time over many years. We were mainly secretaries. There was a presiding angel, bearing the formidable title of 'Warden', who was anything but formidable: Mrs G.S. Taylor was both warm and efficient. How happy she was to recognize our Helena Club in my novel! She wrote to me most affectionately.

The rooms reserved for the youngest girls – those in their teens – held as many as four beds. These were large rooms. The price, including two meals a day, was very modest. I had a room to myself at the top of the house overlooking leafy Kensington Gardens. For this I paid one pound twelve shillings and sixpence per week. If one wanted lunch in the Club, or to give dinner to a guest, that was an extra two shillings and sixpence for each meal.

In 1944 until well after the war food rationing was growing ever tighter. We had ration books which we surrendered to the Club, and they did quite well with difficult food supplies. Sausages, powdered eggs, spam, dried milk, were somehow concocted into a plateful of food followed by apple pudding or cake. Imported food (oranges, lemons, bananas) was not available. But we thought nothing about food, that I remember. Everybody's lot was equal, and lives were being lost everywhere.

At the Helena Club two houses had been made into one. The Club was very spacious with an air of quiet but expensive elegance quite at odds with the humble price we paid. On the ground floor was a large drawing-room leading on to a wide terrace where we could entertain our friends. We had an equally large music room where we could study or play the piano. There were maids to clean the rooms and make our beds. And we were all young and full of fun, despite the war.

On nights when the sirens wailed we would haul our mattresses down to the cellar to sleep there. Sometimes we didn't bother. I was once too lazy to move when I heard the air-raid warning, but I moved quickly enough when a bomb fell nearby breaking my window. Glass flew all over the room but I didn't get a scratch.

I revisited Lancaster Gate some years ago, and for the second time in my life I found that a building I had known was in course of total reconstruction, probably to make a hotel. The Helena Club was gone (as had been the case when I visited my grandparents' former house in Watford).

I had stayed so often in that club in Lancaster Gate, it seemed incredible that it was no more.

One incident in particular stood out in my memory as I stood there in the street: A night of thick London smog, in the black-out. I had arrived at Euston Station from Edinburgh where I had been visiting my family. No taxis were available. I simply didn't know what to do, alone in that blanket fog, totally unable to judge what direction to take. I saw a policeman with a black-out electric torch which had a thick black handle and a dim light that shone inward and downward. I asked him if there would be a bus. – No, they were all taken off the road by the fog, he said. My suitcase was fairly heavy but I lifted it up, ready to walk in any direction the policeman might suggest. He asked me where I lived. 'Bayswater direction,' I said. 'Lancaster Gate.' – 'Let's go,' he said, taking my suitcase. And with the aid of his torch and good sound street-direction, he walked me all the way home. He was very cheerful, and would hardly accept my thank-you. I thought of this as I stood outside that former site of the Helena Club, so many years after.

I lost no time in finding a job. I had extraordinary luck. Soon after arriving in London I registered at the Kensington Public Library and took out some books. One of these was *Elders and Betters* by Ivy Compton-Burnett, for whom I had already formed a great admiration.

The morning after, I went to the local Employment Bureau in Ladbroke Grove to see about a job. I was prepared to take anything. I filled in a form and joined a queue in the secretarial section, armed for a long wait with my copy of Ivy Compton-Burnett.

My turn came. I went into a small office and was asked to sit at a desk, on the other side of which sat a sensible-looking middle-aged woman with a file of cards in front of her. These represented the jobs available. I handed over the completed form. The recruiting administrator, as she was called, meanwhile leaned over and turned my book, which I had laid on the desk, so that she could read the spine. 'Ivy Compton-Burnett,' she said with great enthusiasm. We were soon embarked on a long session of literary talk. I recall that I said Ivy Compton-Burnett resembled the Greek dramatists in her stark themes, and that basically her art was surrealistic. My new friend thought Miss Compton-Burnett one of the most intelligent women writing in English. And so we went on.

When it came to the question of my job, she slid aside her card-index box and took another card out of a drawer, remarking that she imagined I was looking for an interesting job. I said, indeed I was. She asked, would I like to do secret work for the Foreign Office? Long irregular hours. In the country.

She rang up there and then and made an appointment for my interview. I was to go to the very top floor of Bush House in Aldwych. Tell no one. She wished me luck with a lovely smile. I believe I had cheered up her day; she had certainly enlivened mine.

The small office at the top of Bush House was a kind of eyrie overlooking London. The man who interviewed me looked far too big for the room. He was immensely large and fat with a black beard. He was Sefton Delmer, a top newsman of the 'thirties and former European correspondent of the *Daily Express*. His blonde personal assistant, Betty Colbourne, put me at my ease by telling me the sort of work I would have to do, without giving much away about the nature of the job. I would have to be vetted, she said. It would take a few weeks. This meant that the security people would have to look into my past life. I pointed out that this might take a longer time since I had just arrived from Africa.

'Did you come in a convoy?' asked Delmer.

'I don't know,' I said, smiling a little.

It was an elementary test: we had all been warned 'not to know' about the movements of ships and troops, past and present. Great signs were plastered over the walls of public buildings: 'Careless Talk Costs Lives'.

Three weeks passed during which I wandered all over London on foot, savouring the joys of being there, and out of Africa. I had never known London well. Our family visits before the war had been brief. Bombed-out London was the first real London I was to know. I was short of money and badly in need of a job. It troubled me quite a lot that if I didn't get the Foreign Office job I would be in difficulties. There was some doubt, I knew, about my meagre qualifications on paper, but I believe my friend at the Employment Bureau had given me a strong recommendation for natural intelligence. I had been told that I would be unable to tell anyone what sort of work I was doing, but that I could simply declare that I worked in the Foreign Office. In World War II there was always temporary staff in the government departments, but still an aura of privilege clung to the Foreign Office idea. For instance, soon I was able to tell the girl with whom I shared a table in the Helena Club that I had got a job at last; she enquired where, I answered, 'In the Foreign Office,' whereupon she said, 'You must have tons of influence.' I replied that I had no influence at all, just luck. I doubt if she believed me.

The job was wonderfully interesting. I played a very small part, but as a fly on the wall I took in a whole world of method and intrigue in the dark field of Black Propaganda or Psychological Warfare, and the successful and purposeful deceit of the enemy. The entire operation has been described by the late Sefton

Delmer himself in his book *Black Boomerang* (published in 1962 by Secker & Warburg); it is an account of his wartime adventures of the mind and well worth reading.

The Foreign Office secret intelligence service was M.I.6., of which our department was Political Intelligence. I worked in Delmer's Compound at Milton Bryan, near Woburn, which we called M.B. Although he was in complete charge, Delmer's supporters and co-workers included Richard Crossman, Ian Fleming and Bruce Lockhart, all of whom put in appearances from time to time. On the spot, practically day and night, were numerous professors and dons. M.B. was in fact a concentrated brain-tank.

Delmer, then aged forty, had been born and brought up in Berlin where his father was Professor of English at the University. As correspondent for the *Daily Express* during the 'thirties he had met the Nazi leaders frequently. He knew the German mind and spoke German like a native. He was in the best position to run the sort of organization that he founded.

There were two radio stations. First, the Soldiers' Radio Calais (*Soldatensender Calais*) and secondly, in the last phases of the war when I had joined the unit, the powerful Radio Atlantic (*Deutscher Kurzwellensender Atlantik*).

Black propaganda was distinct from the BBC's white variety. Black took up the position that we were loyal Germans devoted to the Führer. From that point of view the news was presented in such a way that the Germans got the impression that they were listening to a German station. This was a camouflage for subtle and deadly anti-Nazi propaganda.

Detailed truth with believable lies: this was outside the scope of the BBC who boasted clearly of our strength, and disparaged the enemy. The methods of Delmer's M.B. unit horrified a few cabinet ministers. Delmer didn't care. His brilliance and ingenuity stimulated admiration, predominantly.

The music we played to the troops was exceptionally good and very popular.

Writing in 1962, Delmer described how, to begin with (in 1941), he had formed a policy to make the Nazi party functionaries

> the number one target of our attack because, in my opinion, the formative and dedicated officials of Hitler's organisation were doing an amazingly effective job as the driving force behind the war effort of the German people. I was immensely impressed by the way Goebbels and his underlings, high and low, were succeeding in cheering and goading the Germans to ever greater effort, and ever greater sacrifices. If we could blacken these men in the eyes of the German public as a venal and slothful privilegenzia which demanded everything from the common man, but made no sacrifices itself, why then we would have struck a mortal blow at a vital nerve of Germany's war morale. Not only that. We would be giving the ordinary German a splendid excuse for any falling short in his own devotion to duty: 'why should I put up with this,' he would be able to say to himself, 'when those party swine can get out of it all.'

Quite a lot of the stories concerned quite ordinary people, but not invented, living at real addresses. This made a convincing effect on the listeners. The names and addresses had been culled by Delmer from the small advertisement columns of the German magazines and newspapers and from the announcements of births, deaths and marriages.

> If I required an engine driver living in the district of Cassel, or a greengrocer's shop in Berlin's Hansa district, my files could provide them ...

Another source of intelligence came from the prisoner of war camps. The walls of their quarters were bugged as were the trees under which they strolled. This yielded the average soldier's state of mind and the latest slang expressions.

Keeping the German army anxious about affairs at home and the German population who listened to this 'German' station worried about the course of the war in the hands of their corrupt leaders, was still daily routine when I joined the unit in 1944. It was always Delmer's joy to find a story he had himself invented being retailed as fact by a POW.

I myself, scanning an English newspaper, found a Delmer-invented story reported as news. This was after D-Day when we were attempting to convince the German troops in Europe to surrender, by always undermining their morale. Slipped between the lines in our propaganda was information that there were no reinforcements coming to them; all had been sent to the Eastern Front; inferior and unreliable foreign troops were fighting there on the Western Front in France with the German troops. The German troops had been particularly conditioned by their own home-distributed propaganda to despise Italian fighters, especially since the Italians had made a separate peace with the Allies the previous year. To fight on the same side as Italians would be decidedly depressing to the German troops.

What I read with great enjoyment in the British newspaper was a straight news item reporting that we, the Allies, now had to employ Italian interpreters to interrogate our POWs because there were so many friendly, pro-Fascist Italians employed on the Western Front as auxiliaries to the *Wehrmacht* (the German army). Of course the story was false. I had seen and heard it invented by Sefton Delmer at his desk in the little newsroom where I occupied the other desk. He had tried it out on me as there was nobody more important around.

In fact, the reason why Delmer called his book *Black Boomerang* was precisely because the techniques of psychological warfare were inclined to turn back on the propagandist. We were constantly in danger of deceiving our own side, and sometimes, at least for a while, we did. But more important, in Delmer's view, was the effect of the black propaganda mythology on the post-war German rationale.

Black propaganda had encouraged the legend of the generals' resistance to the Nazi party. Resistance there certainly was, on 20 July 1944, the day of the bomb plot against Hitler. For two months before the plot our unit had the advantage over the Gestapo of knowing about it, through gossip about Count Stauffenberg, emerging from the German officers who were POWs in their bugged country house camp in England.

At that stage of the war from our 'super-patriotic German' platform it was easy to fool the troops, if not the high-ranking officers. But the generals were incited to read between the lines, and to believe that the Allies would gladly make peace with them and consolidate their leadership, once Hitler and the Nazi party hierarchy were overcome. The Allies, in fact, had no such intentions.

Delmer wrote that in September of that year:

I learned that our broadcasts had indeed been heard by the conspirators, and interpreted in precisely the sense I had hoped. I am sorry the generals ended their lives on Hitler's meat hooks. But I cannot say I have any compunction about having raised false hopes in them. For these men and their caste were the original patrons and sponsors of Hitler's movement. They were the profiteers of his Reich. And they only rose against him when it was clear that he and his war of conquest was doomed.

The radio announcers were Germans, prisoners of war who had agreed to work for us in a role in which, as truly patriotic Germans, they could oppose Hitler and the Nazis. Some were aristocrats, some Communists, some artists and scholars; one POW whom I knew there was a farm-hand who was thoroughly indignant with the SS. They were still POWs in status. We protected them by anonymity. They were known in the compound as 'Otto', 'Kurt' and other names, not theirs. They were to receive British citizenship at the end of the war.

151

Our five-acre compound at Milton Bryan was surrounded by a high mesh-wire and barbed fence with check-point guards on duty day and night. The headquarters was a two-storey red-brick building which looked like a small factory or a barracks. Other buildings, some of them prefabricated, were scattered over the grounds. There was a large red-brick canteen. Deer grazed on the parkland.

My job was that of 'Duty Secretary' to the unit, an opaque definition which somehow fitted in with the untransparent nature of the work.

My hours were generally from four in the afternoon till midnight unless there was a special demand. I was billeted in Woburn in a pleasant old requisitioned rectory together with about five other girls who were part of the unit in various capacities.

I learned to use the 'scrambler' which was a green-painted telephone on which a continual jangling noise made interception difficult. One learned to listen 'through' the jangle. Many of the features we broadcast, in between spells of the really fine dance music, had to do with precise locations that had just been bombed. This was the information I took from the spokesman of the returning crews of the Allied bombers, night after night. I would wait for the right code-name when I answered the phone, then I would say, or the Air Force spokesman would say, 'Shall we go over?' We then went on to the scrambler. (Years later, when I was in India, the ever-present radio music sounded to me just like that scrambler.) The scrambler was located in a different office from where I had my desk. Having taken down the details of the bombing, the number of planes that had gone out and those (not always all) that had returned, I typed out this straight information and gave it to Sefton Delmer. He had an expert staff with an uncanny access to precise streets, houses and cities. It was easy to locate the probable bomb-damage sites in the German cities and make a verifiable story, long before the news was given out on the German radio. And into the bargain might be slipped in a completely false comment about how regrettable it was that the Luftwaffe (the German air force) had now to face penalties for failing to down the Allied planes.

One day in New York in the early 'sixties I met a man in my agent's office whom I felt I had met before. I couldn't place him and he certainly couldn't place me. By careful checking back into the past, it emerged that this man, René de Chochor, had been one of the SHAEF information officers who had phoned me on the scrambler, for so many nights, at M.B. I had remembered the voice although I had never seen the face, never actually 'met' him, in fact.

I had a desk in Delmer's small room next to a marvellous busy newsroom where, by enormous luck, we had a teleprinter directly connected to Goebbels' news transmitter in Germany. This treasure had been inadvertently left behind intact by the London correspondent of the German news network, on his hasty departure at the outbreak of war. The invaluable machine was known as the Hell-schreiber. It enabled us, as Delmer said, 'to put over the poison in our news bulletins without it sounding like enemy propaganda'. Some of the operators of the Hell-schreiber were German Jewish escapees; the work must have given them immense satisfaction.

Besides the scrambler-conveyed information from SHAEF and other armed forces organizations, another nightly call used to reach me from the newsroom of the Foreign Office proper, in Whitehall. This was general news not yet released for the next day's newspapers; we were usually ahead of time. These scrambler conversations would often lapse into the personal, and I was soon on very friendly terms with my colleague, Colin Methven. It proved to be a long and charming friendship.

Colin, like myself, was temporarily separated from his child by the war; his daughter Deirdre had been sent for safety to Canada. Colin and I used to meet in London during my four days' leave every fortnight. In spite of austerity, there was a certain aura about dining at the Savoy, the Ritz, the Café Royal,

Prunier's and other famous restaurants that Colin knew so well. He didn't seem to know the humbler type, and certainly he did his best to make my London leaves a lot of fun. I think he was fairly well off, but the main thing was that he was intensely interesting and had a good sense of humour. We went often to dine before the theatre at the Bath Club, which was one of the London clubs where ladies were allowed, and where Colin's friends would join us. (The Bath Club, having been greatly damaged by a fire, was then housed in the Conservative Club.) I used to love to go to St James's Park with Colin on a Sunday morning, or to the zoo. He was a keen naturalist. He identified every species of duck in the pond. He knew a great deal about rare beasts. Like me, he had been in Central Africa. I now owe to Colin's letters, dating from that time and over the years to come, a great deal of casual information to invigorate my memory.

Of course, we were not permitted to speak of the work we were doing. I never asked Colin about his, nor did he think of enquiring of me about mine. He knew I worked in 'the country', that was all. My letters were sent to me at an address in New Oxford Street and forwarded swiftly to M.B.

My friendship with Colin was not a love affair, and perhaps it was all the better for that. He was a good deal older than me and had been married and divorced twice. He was good-looking, always with a lot of effortless charm, but I think his health had been ruined by a serious wound in the First World War. He had a most dangerous-looking bullet scar in his neck.

I didn't at that time want any romantic attachment, and so Colin, with his delightful conversation, his generous entertainments, his true affection and very sound advice, was always just right for me as he was. I know he enjoyed my company.

I had always been aware of 'gaining experience' for some future literary work. No experience, I felt, was to be overlooked, even that of my darkest hours in Africa. But about the time I met Colin Methven, I felt the need to 'give experience'. I was quite vague in this, although the desire itself was definite. I wanted to offer more of my own personality than hitherto, and give something of the same effect of 'experience' that I received. I wanted to give pleasure through my writings. I longed to write poems and essays or perhaps a play that would be an 'experience' to the reader. I wasn't ready to do so, nor did I have much time in those hard-working days, but I often wrote poems in the mornings while I was working at M.B.

On other mornings, in Bedfordshire, I would go for a walk with a prisoner of war. We were allowed to take those brave POWs, who were risking so much to smash Hitler, for a walk or bicycle ride within a five-mile radius of the compound. What they were risking were denunciations in Germany, or assassination by clandestine POW organizations in England. Of course, if we lost the war ... but that was unthinkable.

The prisoners lived in a house in Woburn Sands with a security officer. They came to work every day on the compound bus, which always stopped at Woburn for me and any other secretary or worker who was on duty; the bus brought us home after midnight. I decided not to attach myself to any one POW as some of the girls had done, but to take them for walks in turns. This proved to be a most interesting way of spending the late morning and early afternoon hours in that lovely spring of 1944. The villagers would look at us with great consternation. Obvious foreigners that our prisoners were, they were regarded as possible spies who had arrived by parachute. But the people had been warned not to approach us with questions. The Germans were not allowed to go into a pub, nor, I think, any other shop. Once I was stopped in the village street with my prisoner by a policeman new on the beat. 'Where do you work?' he said. 'The Foreign Office,' I replied, and indicating my companion (he was Hans, the former farm-hand) I added, 'and this is a distinguished foreign gentleman.' However, after I had shown the policeman my pass and given him a number which he rang from the nearby post office, he went away quite satisfied. 'Only doing my duty, miss.' I feel sure that if he had known that Hans was a

German POW he would almost have fainted. I was glad that Hans himself had not been questioned. He had very little English. We got along mainly with the help of a dictionary. Sometimes Hans, with his survival-savvy, would manage to put together a German picnic of bread, lard and sausages. I would supply bits and pieces to eat. But this man was subject to deep depressions. The roadsides were thickly wooded. Hans said, once, 'Hitler's parachuters will descend here. The woods will be thick with them. They will come.' I knew he only wanted reassurance. I told him that parachutists would hardly choose a wooded area for a landing place, and if they tried to land in the fields we would simply pick them off, one by one.

These were sad words. Our housekeeper at the Old Rectory in Woburn had a son in a parachute regiment. He came to visit her briefly on leave one weekend. I saw him setting off again down the road on foot, past those very woods where lately I had walked with Hans and allayed his fears. The young English soldier jumped to his death at Arnhem shortly afterwards.

Another of my favourite prisoners of war was Kurt, an Austrian count. He wore a shabby red and gold-braid officer's dress coat and a monocle. His English was perfect. Kurt was known as a moving and eloquent broadcaster when we wanted to get a message to the German army on a serious national level. Kurt and I would go round the lovely lanes and pathways of Bedfordshire on foot or sometimes with borrowed bikes. I had drawn a five-mile radius with a compass on a map, but as the signposts of England had all been removed in case of an invasion, we had to judge our itinerary by instinct. Some of my happiest memories go back to those country excursions in the fine spring and summer. The roads were nearly empty of traffic, for petrol-rationing prohibited private transport. In spite of the war, it was good to be in green England after so many years in the parched heat of Africa.

We would talk of 'after the war'. Kurt knew it was only a question of time before Germany was defeated. He understood it was necessary, but he felt genuinely for his people. Although the Allies had taken every precaution to protect the anonymity of the POWs who were working for them, there was always a fear among them of reprisals at home. Kurt would say that if the Nazis had taken his wife he would 'of course' shoot himself.

Some of our prisoners remained in England as British subjects. I got this news in 1948 from one of them, Otto, a young, merry Communist who loathed the Nazis, when I came across him in a newly opened restaurant called The Villa d'Este in the Bayswater Road. He was a waiter. He recognized me first. I looked up and said, 'Otto!' He laughed. His real name was, of course, not Otto.

In the Old Rectory I made friends with other girls who were variously employed at the compound. But as our working hours seldom coincided I saw only one of my billet-mates regularly and daily. This was the oddest relationship I had ever known. Her name was Marcelle Quennell. She was the wife (I believe then separated or divorced) of the writer Peter Quennell, a prominent biographer and literary critic whose name to me, at that time, was God or thereabouts.

Marcelle was very tall and thin, with a small, very white face. She looked as if she had suffered. I believe she was Belgian in origin. Her expression was shrewd and cynical. She accentuated her height by wearing those four-inch cork-soled shoes which were then very fashionable in Paris. They completely spoilt her walk, and took away the natural swing that she had at home in the mornings when she skimmed up and down the stairs.

Marcelle was a good linguist. Her job in the Unit was that of switch-censor. For security a censor sat by a switch during transmissions, following the script which the speaker was broadcasting, and could cut him off if he strayed from the text.

There was always something unexplained and detached about Marcelle. She was over thirty. In the morning it was she who made our coffee in the kitchen. 'Morning' to us was late, due to our hours of work, and so the dreary normal breakfast of rationed tea, toast and margarine would be cleared away before we got down to the large kitchen (in our dressing-gowns, to the housekeeper's horror). I always enjoyed Marcelle's coffee. She stirred it slowly over the gas. Coffee, spurned in those days by the general British population, was off the ration.

Marcelle had moods of grandeur which rather alarmed me. She thought nothing of saying out loud in the hearing of the housekeeper who was supervising the cleaning women in the adjacent scullery, 'After the war *she*'ll have to go back to her semi-detached, roll up her sleeves and work.' And it annoyed Marcelle intensely that the housekeeper referred to the cleaners as 'my women'. I took those people's pretensions as fun, but Marcelle didn't. In turn, the good lady would inveigh against Marcelle in her absence. 'Bossy foreigner. And dragged through the divorce courts.' I remember remarking that I, too, was divorced; there had been no dragging. But the housekeeper seemed not to hear what I said. She had it in for Marcelle only.

Marcelle's grand manner sometimes vented itself on me. 'I don't know how you can exist in England without a private income,' she declared. 'I have three hundred a year and they take off half for unearned income tax.' Another time she pointed out that I was occupying a room to myself instead of sharing, although I was only twenty-six. 'Private rooms are for people over thirty.' I had never met anyone like her. I knew she was unbalanced. I told her once on an impulse that I was sorry for her, and I meant it sincerely. It was in no way a patronizing remark. Marcelle's face crumpled a bit. 'No need to be sorry for me,' she muttered. A little while later, with a nice expression on her face, she brought me a bar of French soap. (Soap was tightly rationed and good soap unobtainable.) I remember her standing in the doorway of my room on that occasion. 'Goodness,' I said spontaneously. 'You look like Mary Queen of Scots.'

'You're not the first person to say that. What makes you think so?'

'Just an impression,' I said. She did indeed have something in her looks of the Scottish Queen's portraits.

I thought, privately, that she was rather a security risk. But of course that wasn't my department.

One of the prisoners, a very tall, good-looking, rather reckless type, had become Marcelle's temporary boyfriend. They were obviously having a romantic affair, to say the least.

One day that prisoner was missing. He had been sent back to the POW camp for a variety of reasons, mainly, I suppose, general indiscipline. Of course he was under strict surveillance. It was in his own interests not to talk to his fellow prisoners about where he had been, and why. He was, besides, still bound by the Official Secrets Act, and knew it. But it happened that the Red Cross or some such international organization had arranged through the BBC and the German state radio a reciprocal prisoners' 'Hallo, Folks' programme – the voice of 'our Billie', POW in Germany, telling his family in Oldham that he was safe and well in exchange for 'our Fritz', POW in England, telling his family in Cologne the same thing.

Our erstwhile collaborator, Marcelle's friend, now volunteered for one of these broadcasts. Our security surveillance slipped up and his voice, which had hitherto broadcast on our Radio Calais, now went over the air in the prison-camp context. It was recognizable as a voice, and traceable. Whether that fool's voice was, in fact, ever recognized, or his identity traced to his family (with almost certain reprisals), I never heard. But there was a tremendous fuss, with Marcelle stalking around sulkily for a while, at the same time looking for someone new.

I used this incident with fictional variations in my novel *The Hothouse by the East River*. There was something surrealistic, mysterious, about the affair, which I think the novel tones in with.

Marcelle took her own life some time after the war. I felt very sad indeed when I read about it in a newspaper paragraph. Strange, proud Marcelle! I feel she must have suffered, mentally, beyond endurance, even before the period when I knew her. She was one of those people whom there is little one can do to help. She was already, when I met her, on the other side of some invisible barrier which only a stray word of sympathy or a tablet of rare French scented soap could, for a moment, pass over. Was her despair due to drugs? Drink? Men? Or merely the brittle condition of being Marcelle that pushed her to that last extremity? I have never forgotten, I cannot forget her.

Mostly, on my trips to London every two weeks I put up at the Helena Club. Sometimes I went to stay at Shiplake, near Henley-on-Thames, where my friend from Rhodesia, May Heygate, was now living with her father-in-law. She had returned to England shortly before me and was now preparing to marry her husband's brother, who was fighting in France. The Church of England would not allow this union, so she eventually had a civil marriage. When I went to stay, we often made trips to London together, especially on Monday mornings, since I had to catch a train back to the country in the evening. There I made friends, through May, with a popular singer, Jack Cooper. He was on the BBC, a performer (in fact he was a 'crooner') with a regular feature every weekday at five in the afternoon with 'Fred Hartley's Quartet'. I saw quite a lot of him when, after that, I went to London and wasn't seeing Colin Methven. My London days were more or less enjoyable in spite of the V1s, robot planes that fell with a warning from June onwards, and the subsequent V2s that started to land without warning in September. It was amusing to hear Jack Cooper crooning pre-arranged songs especially for me when I was back at work at the compound. He had quite a good voice, church-trained.

Nineteen years later exactly, I had a letter from Jack Cooper. He had been reading my books with pleasure and wanted to know if I was the same 'strange, sweet, little red-headed creature with a burning ambition to become a writer whom he had known during the war?' He added, very truly, 'With the hectic life of those days we drifted apart.' We met again and enjoyed talking about what were already, for us, old times.

At the Helena Club my friends there would come to my room after dinner to talk and make coffee. Sometimes we had sherry, a precious present from Colin. My best friend in the club, Pamela Flood, a very beautiful girl, used to like me to read her my latest poems. She was a good judge and critic of poetry.

If my leave had been cancelled at any fortnight's end for some exigency (such as the Invasion of Europe) I would collect eight days' leave after a month's steady work. This would give me time to slip up to Edinburgh for a spell to see my family. The passenger trains, of course, had to give way to troop transport, and so, frequently, one arrived seven or eight hours late – a journey of fifteen hours or more. It was seldom one got a seat. I don't know how we had the stamina, but we did.

One night, on the return journey, I got talking to a girl on the train who was returning to her job as an *au pair* children's help in north London. I imagined I would have to spend the night in the station. But my travelling companion pressed me to come home with her and spend the night at St John's Wood. Her employers, 'the Professor' and his wife, were away, and the house was empty. I readily accepted. Those sort of invitations were not uncommon during the war.

The house was near Lord's cricket ground. After I was indoors a short while, I discovered, from looking at the inscriptions on the interesting poetry books ('Louis from Wystan' etc.), that 'the Professor' was the poet Louis MacNeice. I was anxious then, lest he and his wife should come home and find me there. But my friend reassured me of that. I slept in a Morrison shelter. This was a steel-canopied bed built inside the house. I was extremely impressed to look at the desk, the pens, the books of Louis MacNeice. I have written about it in an essay

'The Poet's House' and the experience is also the basis of my short story 'The House of the Famous Poet'.

I felt I had truly entered the world of literature; it had symbolically materialized; it was real.

CHAPTER SIX

The year after the war I found a job on a good quarterly magazine called *Argentor*. I have no idea, and my records do not say, how I got this job. Presumably I applied for it through a newspaper advertisement, but I can't be sure of this. At the Helena Club, where I stayed, there was always a grapevine about available jobs the girls had heard of, so it is possible that one of my friends at the Club put me on to *Argentor*.

My son Robin had arrived from Africa in the previous autumn and I had been in Edinburgh settling him into his new home and school. There was not only very little scope for me in Edinburgh to earn my living, but it was not at all convenient that I should continue to live with my parents, especially as they had taken responsibility for my son. I had waived all claim to alimony in his interests. From then on I lived in London and visited Edinburgh as often as I could. My addiction to the telephone started at this time; I was always calling home to my family, or they calling me. For a while I was sent by the Foreign Office – 'seconded' was the word – to the US War Information Service in Inveresk House in London. This was pleasant, but now in a stage of winding up. *Argentor* was my first literary job.

Argentor was a beautifully produced magazine, resembling the *Connoisseur* in style and format, the official quarterly journal of the National Jewellers' Association. My job was mainly research in museums, libraries, art galleries: a truly refreshing occupation. I loved it. Even now, looking at the list of contents of the first number in which I was involved, the pleasure of that work comes back to me. The editor, William Llewellyn-Amos, was particularly trusting, and quite uncaring about my lack of experience. His confidence in me was stimulating. I had no hesitation about writing contributions on a subject hitherto unknown to me. Another journalist, Mona Curran, was employed in the office; we worked together well. Quite a lot of articles by specialists had to be touched up from the stylistic point of view, and we spent long hours recasting the articles that had been commissioned.

The list of contents in the number under preparation when I joined the magazine included an article on English domestic silver, and one on spoons and forks; another was 'Old Clocks of England' and James Gunn, a celebrated portrait painter, contributed 'Jewels and the Painter'. The journal, very well illustrated, aimed to express high standards of workmanship, and to give the readers an idea of the history of the jewellers' art, and that of goldsmiths, silversmiths, horologists and the allied crafts. One of my first assignments was to work on an article (signed by the editor) called 'The Goldsmith Painters', relating how many of the Renaissance artists began as goldsmiths. On my own account, I wrote 'Some Jewels of English Poetry', in which I showed how the names of jewels were used figuratively throughout English poetry. (To my surprise and joy this article was picked out for a highly favourable mention by the *Evening Standard*: my stock in the office went up.) Later on, before I left *Argentor*, I had researched and written a long article on the Order of the Golden Fleece which adorns many famous and historical portraits. About this article I have a sense of great satisfaction. It bears no signs of immaturity and I would not hesitate to reprint it today.

The number of subjects connected with the goldsmiths', silversmiths' and jewellers' art was inexhaustible. The essays written by experts which needed some form of recasting were mainly passed on to me. I learned how to copy-edit tactfully. I recall that I took out a great many adjectives.

My working days were long. I spent hours on research at the College of Arms, the National Gallery, the British Museum and similar institutions. Further hours were spent in the office, writing and editing. And sometimes I would work at home on an interesting article, far, far into the night.

I got no extra pay for work I had done at home, and of my own composition. I wasn't expected to sell my work to the magazine, for I 'belonged' to the magazine. Even when I wrote a small poem, much approved of by the editor, this too went in with my wages, six pounds a week, as a matter of course. I was perfectly happy with this arrangement. I enjoyed the work and was learning, too, how to edit a magazine, and how to proof-read and copy-edit. *Argentor* continued to publish my work (no pay) till 1948, two years after I left, and was editing the *Poetry Review* for the Poetry Society. But *Argentor* is no more. It is now an expensive production often quoted in the rare book lists.

I took over from the ancient editor of the *Poetry Review* (journal of the Poetry Society), Galloway Kyle, in the spring of 1947. I was now aged twenty-nine.

My friend from the Foreign Office, Colin Methven, had gone to live with his sister in Perthshire, while his daughter, Deirdre, commuted between Perth and London. Colin was still, and was to remain, my principal moral support. We had a voluminous correspondence and he encouraged me to telephone to him 'reverse charges' (collect), which I frequently did. But I missed Colin's presence in London. Deirdre, too, wrote frequently, for although she was devoted to Colin she felt the need of more freedom than he felt he could allow her. I saw both points of view, probably Deirdre's more than Colin's. Occasionally Deirdre would have a dance in London arranged for her, when Colin would put in an appearance. I was always invited to those dances and small parties, in the fashionable night spots of London. But for the most part I was lonely. I had left the Helena Club for a while and taken furnished rooms (with a shilling-in-the-slot gas meter) in Clarges Street, and then Half Moon Street, off Piccadilly. But I felt lonelier than ever, and soon went back to the Helena Club. It was full of noisy and cheerful chatter and I sometimes found it difficult to work there – but at least I had my friends in the evenings, not to mention those square meals that were prepared for us.

The Poetry Society, the scene of my next job, today, incredibly, possesses no trace of any of its archives or files that date back to the foundation of the Society in 1909, nor, of course, to the period 1947–49 when I was employed, or rather embroiled, in that then riotous establishment. The present kindly director, Chris Green, and his staff have done their utmost to trace for me documentary evidence of my even having been there. The magnificent library is safe and well displayed in the University of York, I am told, but all documents have been lost. (There were said to have been wax gramophone recordings of Tennyson, much deteriorated, but I never saw them at the Poetry Society's offices in Portman Square.) No trace, so far, of past relics or documents has appeared in any of the university collections which normally take care of important archives, although it is always possible that some of the correspondence at least lies stagnant in some private collection. It is thought, however, that the files were simply destroyed during successive moves, first from Russell Square to Portman Square (where I worked), and later to Earls Court Square where the Society functions precariously at present.

I asked Anthony Whittome, a recent official of the Poetry Society, if he knew anything about those long-ago years 1947–49 when I was trying to run it. He writes,

On your general points about the 'lively time' of 1947–49, all I can say is *plus ça change*! The poetry world seems inherently faction-ridden and fissiparous, and the Society has had quite a few public squabbles even in the years I was involved.

Fortunately I have guarded a number of documents and letters of my own to assist my memory.

I had joined the Poetry Society in 1946 as a member, after seeing an advertisement for a reading to be held on its premises in Portman Square.

In the May 1947 issue of the Society's bi-monthly journal, the *Poetry Review*, I won the first prize in a Love Lyric competition with a metaphysical sonnet. 'It has an air about it. It is a lovely poem,' wrote the judge. Re-reading the poem I am sure it has an air about it, but certainly it was merely an old-fashioned exercise in what I thought would win that poetry prize.

The adjudicator was, as I learned, T. Christmas Humphreys (later Judge), who became a lifelong friend. His father, Mr Justice (Sir Travers) Humphreys, was a High Court judge, one of the 'hanging judges' of those dire days.

Toby, as Christmas Humphreys was known to his friends, was an extremely helpful support in the stormy times to come, not only with sound legal advice, but with warm friendship which, as it turned out, I needed greatly. Puck, his wife, was equally friendly and hospitable. Toby writes in his memoirs of those days (*Both Sides of the Circle*) – days and months, when factions in the Poetry Society for and against practically everything, were implacably lined up in opposition,

> ... there was trouble in the Poetry Society, then housed in its eighteenth-century premises in Portman Square. Founded by the Chevalier Galloway Kyle twenty years earlier, the society had built up a very fine membership and library. The time came for Kyle to retire and his successor was the unwitting cause of immediate trouble. While running competitions for the *Poetry Review* I had twice presented the prize to a Mrs Muriel Spark. She was now elected as General

Secretary and editor of the Review. This young, extremely
attractive Scot, who possessed charm, ebullience and office
efficiency, proved to be, through no fault of her own, more of a
Chinese cracker than a new broom. Soon, indeed, she was
staying with Puck and me as almost a refugee from the storm
in Portman Square. How the storm died down I do not
remember, but Sparklet, as we knew her, went on to become a
famous novelist.

Another friend from those days from whom I have solicited
comments, the poet John Heath-Stubbs, has merely replied,
'You were too avant-garde for them.'

But it was not all as simple as that. It was much more elaborate.

I was offered the job of General Secretary of the Society and
Editor of the *Review* for the pay of thirty pounds per month plus
a free flat in the premises at 33 Portman Square. I accepted on the
basis of the flat. I wanted a home. My son was now nine years old;
and I thought it would be a fine thing if he could go to a prep
school nearby and be with me more often. Colin Methven was
enthusiastic about the idea; he had in store in London a complete
houseful of furniture (including pots and pans) and his letters
tell how much trouble he went to for me, with his lists and
arrangements, after I had taken on the job. I gave it a few
months' trial before acting. Then, with the Council's approval, I
arranged for the first packing cases to be delivered to the Poetry
Society offices at Portman Square. I also found a prep school in
Sussex which seemed to me within my means and that of Robin's
educational allowance from his father. My son was keen on the
move to be near me.

Then two things immediately happened. First, the Poetry
Society started to dither about the flat. I quite understood that
the former editor and his wife, an elderly couple, the Galloway
Kyles, should not be put out of their home, but there was another
flat available, casually and nominally let to an affluent couple in
no way connected to the Society. I do not think they were even

given notice to quit, for by that time trouble had arisen about the editorial policy of the *Poetry Review*. The second thing was that my ex-husband raised objections through his lawyers about Robin leaving Edinburgh.

I never got the flat. And I now realized that I had been elected to the job on the assumption that I could be manipulated, whereas I took up the position that if you are in the driver's seat, you drive.

Simultaneously with my appointment the annual subscription to the Society was doubled from ten shillings to a pound, and the price of the *Poetry Review*, if sold separately, was raised from two shillings and sixpence to four shillings and sixpence. This was a challenge. Members who could not afford the new subscription resigned and the increased revenues were expected to balance the difference. On the whole, I believe this did happen.

Before taking on the *Review* I had stipulated that contributors should be paid, thus raising the quality of the *Review* which had been poor and amateurish. A great deal of rage had been vented against 'the moderns'. The following is an example of the *Poetry Review* criticism (June–July 1946) before I took over.

> It is an encouragement to encounter a book which evinces, by comparison with earlier volumes by the same person [Geoffrey Grigson] an improvement not merely of technique but in that fundamental attitude towards poetry which can become so heretical and subversive.

My first editorial, in a magazine with a new format, began 'Cannot we cease railing against the moderns?' This encouraged the poets but left some of the readers disconsolate. Up to now, Eliot, Pound, Auden, had been dirty words.

It emerged that numerous contributors had been virtually paying for publication. Among these was Miss Alice Hunt Bartlett of New York who had hitherto contributed a regular review of American poetry. As an example of her taste, I quote from the same issue of *Poetry Review*, where she cites a 'startling stanza' of a poem in which the 'littleness of man is constantly revealed against the mighty background of the universe':

> I see a new America
> Not far along the track
> Where earth rides steeplechase with death
> Across the zodiac.

Miss Bartlett sent me some pages of equivalent rubbish with a cheque for twenty-five dollars made out in my name. I passed this over to the Treasurer, John Graddon, who handled the Society's funds and paid the bills. But he said it would have to be made out in the Society's name, and anyway, he suspected the money was intended for me, personally. I sent it back to Miss Bartlett at the same time as I rejected the piece. She wrote again, saying that her cheques had always been welcomed by the previous editor, and she had 'visioned' a close co-operation between us. She had also 'visioned' a Poets' Day with a procession including poets on a series of floats moving in triumph up Fifth Avenue.

Before long I had difficulties with a very active member of the Executive Committee of the Society. This was Robert Armstrong, a physically and morally twisted, small, dark fellow, a veritable nightmare. I had published a poem of his which had been accepted by the previous editor and which I could decently stand by – it was not too bad. But I didn't think his name worth a mention on the front cover. I announced a list of contributors 'and others'. The subsequent correspondence still, after forty-five years, chills me with its petty implication and with his vanity. He wrote to me – as he always did, on writing paper headed H.M. Inspector of Taxes, Willesden District – on 9 December 1947, a long letter from which I extract:

After your suggestion and then your promise, in the Evening you met Sir Eugene [*sic*] Millington Drake, I was surprised to find myself among the 'others' on the cover; (although I am glad you have some well known names despite their limited contributions in some instances.)

It rather hamstrings my own undertaking that I would then be able to use the 'Review' for a drive through Civil Service organs or elsewhere (where my identity has been screened behind 'Critic', 'Spectator', 'Dunrobin Goodfellow', or 'Observer' etc.) I had been working hard for the opportunity to put the Society and yourself on the map – and the added recognition would have assisted. I had also put in some groundwork with influential friends so I am puzzled and assume something must have arisen to sidetrack your promise.

This was a mere taste of things to come. I made a lasting enemy of Robert Armstrong then and there. I replied:

I did not promise that your name would appear on the front cover of 'Poetry Review', and if you thought I did you misunderstood me. It does not seem to me to be a matter upon which one 'promises'. . . . I do not give names of contributors prominence in order to please or promote the status of the contributor, but to enhance the value of 'Poetry Review'.

You say that you have written in Civil Service journals under pseudonyms. Thus, if I were to give prominence to your real name (under which you have not written much and are little known) it would not help me in my aims, nor do I see how it would 'put Poetry Review on the map' as you say in your letter.

I ended this letter on a note of sheer placatory hypocrisy.

I have 'Poetry Review' at heart and this I place before all personalities, even those as pleasant and charming as yourself.

However, I never in future put this man's name on the front cover, on which I announced work by poets who had at least published a book of verse. With the exception of a very few, such as Roy Campbell, Alex Comfort, John Heath-Stubbs, the majority were destined not to last, but they were the best I could get.

Robert Armstrong contributed a poem to one of his Civil Service journals which badly plagiarized the work of another, rather fine poet, Arnold Vincent Bowen. When this was discovered by sheer accident, and Armstrong was confronted with it, he explained that he was trying to put the poet 'on the map'.

I must say something here about Sir Eugen Millington-Drake, mentioned in Armstrong's letter. He was a former ambassador, a very pleasant man of about sixty, my parents' generation. He took me frequently to the theatre, which I loved, and which his wife Lady Effie didn't care for. Eugen supported me entirely throughout the ensuing strife at the Poetry Society. He was a Vice-President. His interest in me was by no means romantic. Indeed, to the bewilderment of some members of the Council (Armstrong and his friends), Effie used often to pick up Eugen and me and drop us off at the theatre in her chauffeur-driven car.

'Have a good time,' she would say. These aristocratic airs appalled and shocked my puritanical bourgeois opponents. Eugen gave some poetry readings which it was my job to organize weekly. He read beautifully.

When Eugen took me for dinner I used to love to hear his stories of how the Battle of the River Plate was won by a stroke of diplomatic bluff. Eugen had been, in fact, responsible for the scuttling of the *Graf Spee* in 1939 when he was British Minister at Montevideo.

(Many years later, in the early 'seventies in Rome, I found to my pleasure that the Millington-Drakes had the flat above mine in the Palazzo Taverna. I used to slip up to Effie for tea whenever I wanted a tea. I am fond of their son, Teddy, who lives near me in Tuscany – a very close friend.)

There is something about a passion for poetry that brings out a primitive reaction, especially in non-poets, that is, the 'poetry lovers'. Anthony Whittome's words, quoted above, 'The poetry world seems inherently faction-ridden and fissiparous . . . ', seem undeniably true when I look at those of my documents, reports and letters that I fortunately rescued from oblivion when I left the Society.

An anonymous letter now reached the wife of the Chairman of the Society. It fell short of the mark, since it accused me of running around the West End at night with her husband, whereas the good woman knew quite well he was home every night. He was an elderly, home-loving type. I had sometimes been out to lunch with him. I didn't see eye to eye with his reactionary ideas about poetry and we didn't get on so very well on that score. But I was prepared to be patient.

The question was, who had sent the anonymous letter? I wanted to hand it to the police, but the general feeling, on the advice of Toby Humphreys, the best of all legal experts on our Executive Committee, was to ignore it. We had two main suspects amongst the grievance-bearers, but no proof.

Young poets had begun to drop in to see me at Portman Square. The Society's offices were in a pretty Georgian house. I occupied a small room on the ground floor opposite a large office where Miss Cracroft, the Registrar, and two helpers worked. Miss Cracroft, known as Cray, was a handsome middle-aged woman; she looked after auditions for a gold-medal examination in elocution that was held every year for schoolchildren. It was a profitable venture and brought a good income into the Society. I left that side to Cray. She also took charge of the subscriptions and the banking. The office ran itself. I hardly ever went into the big office. A secretary called Barbara would take letters in short-hand whenever I needed her, which was seldom, and she typed the minutes of the executive meetings which I attended as Secretary of the Society. But I devoted my main energies to the *Review*.

The young poets were full of hope that there would now be a place for them in the newly organized magazine. I did make a place for a number of them. There was no outstanding talent, but the type of verse they wrote was totally different from what had gone before. Irregular rhythms, strange ideas, free modes of expression were what enraged quite a lot of the former readers, although by no means all. One of my most staunch supporters was an eighty-two-year-old widower, Brigadier General Sir George Cockerell (who, as a young man, had heard Liszt play). He used to invite me, with other younger people of his acquaintance, artists, writers and singers, to his lovely house at Hyde Park Corner for dinner. I suppose this caused envy among the people he didn't invite. But he liked amusing people, and could not stand bores.

The young poets brought me poetic tributes – poems dedicated to myself – which I lapped up contentedly without letting them influence me in the slightest.

One enraged reader who joined in the campaign of harassment against me was Dr Marie Stopes, the famous birth control expert – on that account, much to be admired. She was absolutely opposed to my idea of poetry. Up to his death three years earlier she had been living with Lord Alfred Douglas, the fatal lover of Oscar Wilde, an arrangement which I imagine would satisfy any woman's craving for birth control. I met her at one of our meetings and knew she disliked me intensely on sight. I was young and pretty and she had totally succumbed to the law of gravity without attempting to do a thing about it.

She wrote me a bitchy letter to ask me, was it true my husband had divorced me. I wrote back telling her to mind her own business; my private life had nothing to do with my work. She wrote back (27 May 1948):

... as a Vice President and a member long concerned for the good name of the Poetry Society, I am fully entitled to be informed and to make enquiries about yourself.

Mr Harding [a former Chairman] told me that your husband had divorced you. I enquired of another person why I had been misinformed by him and not told this fact.

I request you to inform me whether or not your husband divorced you ...

I wrote back (29 May 1948):

I have received your outrageously impudent letter of 27th May.

My private affairs are no concern of yours and your malicious interest in them seems to me to be most unwholesome. You have no rights whatsoever to make enquiries about me – all enquiries necessary were made by those who appointed me and confirmed my appointment. I must say that your attitude fills me with contempt, as it would all right-thinking people.

I heard no more directly, but indirectly she did what damage she could.

I calculated, anyway, that the worst damage anyone could do me in that frustrated environment was to cause me to lose my job. I had begun to feel the job was not worth it, for I wasn't able to move into the flat I had been promised. But I was determined to work well so long as I held the position of editor.

Perhaps my most annoying contestant was a banker and amateur literary man of sixty, William Kean Seymour, a born mediocrity. He told me he had himself very much wanted the job of editor and had been disappointed when it came to me. I had occasion to remind him of this in later letters, fortunately salvaged by me. Kean Seymour had written some books of poetry.

My first encounters with him were very cordial. He would call into the office and if I had time I would go round the corner for a cup of tea with him. He was married to a novelist, Rosalind Wade, whom I met at a dinner party. She treated me with eloquent coldness. Kean Seymour came round the next day in a state of agitation, apologizing for his wife. I asked him what was the matter. He said he had been unable to sleep at nights and had spent those nights walking up and down some corridor or gallery, because he had been thinking of me. He had told his wife all about it.

I told him he had better inform her that his feelings for me were not reciprocated and that he was putting me in a false position. But this seemed to please him. I got him out of the office and wrote a letter to his wife telling her plainly that I didn't want her husband and that I already had a boyfriend (which was true). I have no record of Rosalind Wade's reply but I gained the distinct impression that she was more annoyed that I didn't want her husband than if I did.

William Kean Seymour saw my letter and came bursting into my office demanding to know if it was true that I had a boyfriend, and who he was.

I told him. It was Howard Sergeant, a young accountant and poet who was active in the Poetry Society and who edited a magazine of his own called *Outposts*. Howard had been my boyfriend since I first went to work at the Poetry Society, among so many unspeakable people. One big attraction of Howard was that he danced so beautifully. I loved to go dancing with him and often did. Another attraction was that he was fairly manly.

William Kean Seymour turned totally against me from that day. In no other job have I ever had to deal with such utterly abnormal people. Yes, it is true, poetry does something to them.

Kean Seymour had written to me after the publication of my first number, griping about the absence from it of one of his articles. In one of the frantic letters I have now before me, he put his complaint on to his friends – they had 'looked in vain' for his piece. 'So many people have expressed pleasure in my more or less regular articles that it seems to me a pity to disappoint them.' I tried in vain to placate him. But that fellow would come into the office behaving as if it was his own domain. I repeatedly asked him not to do so. He accused me of holding 'underground meetings'. He assured me that he was 'not an ally'. I replied that we were all in the office extremely busy. We were short-staffed. I wrote snootily:

> I have had reason to complain on several occasions of your manner of lifting and reading papers which happen to be lying on my desk, and of giving instructions to my staff without permission. ... If you wish to see me, please telephone and make an appointment.

I had often found him in the busy working office taking tea with the staff, pumping them for information which was by no means secret or sensational. Cray and the two girls were simply polite, but puzzled. I reminded Kean Seymour there were over three thousand members and subscribers to the magazine. I had to be concerned for all their rights, not those of one in particular.

The printers came to see me in bewilderment. Did they take orders from me or from a Mr Robert Armstrong? He had come to question them about the magazine.

And so it went on. I wonder what an intelligent young woman today would do in such circumstances. I hated to have 'allies'. My supporters were all leading normal lives. The more talented poets and intelligent people like Sir George Cockerell, the Treasurer, John Graddon, the Librarian, H.K. Grant, Toby Humphreys, Eugen Millington-Drake, Mrs Violet Adamson, Dom Ambrose Agius OSB and many others and, as it turned out later, people prominent in the literary establishment, were far too civilized to plot and plan the downfall of an opposition in a cultural society. It would not have occurred to them, far less to me, to write letters to the Presidents of the Society, first Lord Wavell then Lord David Cecil, bombarding them with complaints, as did those disappointed poets, resentful of anything new. The Presidents never turned up at meetings; their positions were purely nominal. Naturally, a great many people resigned in my support when I left rather than engage in further turmoil.

General meetings would often be led by Marie Stopes literally shaking her fist and making inflammatory, wild pronouncements. I think she was demented at this stage of her life. I used to think it a pity that her mother rather than she had not thought of birth control. On one occasion the Chairman's wife brandished her umbrella in Dr Stopes' face. 'Mabel, Mabel!' called her husband. 'Stop it at once. Sit down.' Although all of the Society's three thousand members were not waving their rejection-slips in over-heated indignation, it did seem to me and my friends that a great many were doing so. Numerous members seemed to think their increased subscription had bought space in the magazine for their poetry. I learned that to be an editor you have to be completely independent in fact as well as intention.

I thought wistfully of *Argentor*, also a society's journal, and yet so interesting and of such a high standard. But I knew that when I left the *Poetry Review* at least it could not, for a long time, return to the poor parish-magazine level at which I had found it.

On 29 August 1948, writing to a new member of the Council who was extremely sympathetic and asked me for my views, I wrote that the dissatisfied groups were:

a. People who fundamentally resent a young woman in authority, and especially when their own work is being judged.

b. People who themselves wish to edit *Poetry Review*. There are two, of whom I am definitely aware, on the Council.

I have tried hard to exercise tact with these members and have succeeded in some cases. For more than a year I have been tactful and charming until my face aches of it. . . . There is a constant re-grouping of sides and it seems to me the aims of the Society are being forgotten.

The name of this new member was Collin Brookes. Strangely, I cannot recall his face as I can that of most people, and vividly, after forty-four years. I remember only his completely reasonable and unruffled attitude, which was outstanding in that environment.

(I wrote the above, as I wrote all personal and semi-personal letters, on my own writing paper, because Robert Armstrong had raised the petty question in a council meeting, whether I used Poetry Society paper for letters to my supporters in the Society and therefore at the Society's expense. I could have pointed out that he wrote all his letters about his poems and Poetry Society business on Inland Revenue government paper, in other words at the taxpayer's expense, but I didn't feel I could sink quite so low.)

I had already started looking for a better job. Colin Methven wrote from Perthshire, advising me strongly not to resign. I had kept him closely informed. His packing cases were still piled up in Portman Square, but I agreed at a committee meeting, and it was recorded in the minutes that I agreed, that we should not evict the previous editor, and only await the outcome of negotiations for the other flat (which was the one I had been promised). In fact I had been thoroughly tricked, and Colin Methven, among many, was well aware of it. He felt, as did Toby Humphreys, that if I resigned I would sacrifice my right even to severance pay. I chose to be dismissed rather than resign, much to the Chairman's annoyance, for I then got three months' pay when, in his words, the Society 'terminated the services of the editor.' Three months was little enough. Colin wanted me to stand out for far more. This was on the advice of his solicitor, whom he had consulted.

But I was delighted to get out of that scene of strife and of that mortal sin of art, pomposity. I went to stay at the Humphreys'. All the main newspapers were informed by my opponents of their version of the story, but they invariably backfired, and the story was reported unfavourably to the Society, the remaining members of which were furious. There had been, with my leaving, a considerable exodus of poets, good and bad. (I must admit that a great many of the men and women who gave me their devoted allegiance were very feeble writers.)

Answering the questions of the press about the list of resignations from the Poetry Society, the Chairman put it: 'There was a slight difference of opinion about the retention or non-retention of Mrs Spark ... '

But differences of opinion continue to this day. Even as I write, arrives a press cutting dated 27 January 1992 from the *Daily Telegraph*, headed: PRESIDENT QUITS IN POETRY SOCIETY ROW. (The row is about the purchase of new premises for the Society.)

With the help of Toby Humphreys and a group of breakaway poets I founded a new magazine, *Forum*. This was well received in the papers, but it couldn't continue long without a subsidy. However, by that time I had a new full-time job and was replanning my life. I broke entirely with my boyfriend of eighteen months, Howard Sergeant.

Howard was a travelling accountant and was often away. He had been a staunch supporter of the *Poetry Review*, although often, I thought, rather too interfering. He was an extremely jealous man. He loathed my friend, the good Treasurer of the Society, John Graddon, and felt he could do the job better. More than anything, according to the hundreds of letters he sent me and which I find among my papers, he disliked what he called my 'liking for male company'. I was unable to take this as seriously as he evidently meant it. I agreed heartily that I liked male company, especially as I lived in a club with at least sixty girls. I told him I also liked the company of women who liked male company. But Howard's letters expressed his own lack of confidence. He swore eternal love but was upset because, for instance, I had told him that if any relationship interfered with my natural bond with my son I would break the relationship. He brooded on this. He set up quarrels with any other eligible men I merely went out with. He confronted one of them at home, at eight in the morning.

I am told by independent readers that the love poems he wrote me are quite good. I don't know about that. They are written to an egocentric idea, or an impossible ideal. He didn't begin to know me. He himself was in his early thirties, married and getting a divorce. The divorce had not proceeded as far as he had led me to believe. Howard wrote a long anguished letter describing a scene with his wife in which he had 'told' her. He repeated a lot of her arguments against their divorce, many of which I thought perfectly sound, especially when she pointed out to him that I would never be able to keep his house clean without assistance which he could not afford. I was, in fact, distressed to be dragged into a sordid business I had imagined was virtually all settled.

Twice, when Deirdre Methven asked me to bring someone along to one of her dances, I took Howard. He was presentable enough, tall and fair, but he didn't go down well with the Methven party. Colin didn't think him right for me. My parents thought he wasn't 'good enough'. I sensed that my son, Robin, although he said nothing, would never care for him. One day I woke up and decided I didn't like him, either. I had good reason.

Howard's favourite words were 'integrity' and 'compassion'. He was forever invoking these attributes. If, coming out of a night spot, he couldn't persuade a cab to take us home, he would shout at the driver, 'Have you no compassion?' By this time I knew that I could never marry Howard, on the grounds of his deficient sense of humour alone.

'Integrity . . . compassion . . . ' In fact, he had neither. Shortly after I had left the stormy Poetry Society and was settling down to my new job (on a periodical called *European Affairs*), and was also attending to my own much-neglected writings, I had the nastiest, meanest letter (21 April 1949) from Howard that it is conceivable to imagine, especially in contrast to his previous voluminous effusions of love and admiration. I believe I had already told him that I could not tie myself permanently to him, but that I could be a friend. Perhaps this rankled. Now that I could no longer be of use to him on the *Poetry Review* he accused me of past arrogance. 'You attempted to ride roughshod over me', etc. Now, he wrote, 'You like to sit back and dream of the past glory.' It was a very distasteful outburst; he gloated and jeered where previously he had flattered. He had, in fact, already said a few decidedly nasty things on those lines, in conversation, which I found quite awful. Even if he had been right about my 'arrogance' (which in fact was only editorship), his was a street-corner attitude. I thought it petty, low. But now, I was thoroughly amazed by that phrase, 'dream of the past glory'. He meant the *Poetry Review*. I was at this moment thinking of publishing books in the future. I had no intention of making a career out of my job. And it struck me, that Sergeant's ambitions were betraying him. I knew he was ambitious, but I had not realized how the intensity of an ambition could be out of all proportion to its object. 'Glory' was how he thought of that frightful ill-paid job I had just left. The best magazines at that time were in any case *Horizon* and *Poetry London*, both excellent. But to him the Poetry Society journal was 'glory'.

Shortly after this I arranged to edit, jointly, a book of essays on Wordsworth to celebrate the centenary of his death in 1850. Howard rang me up in a great stew, claiming that I was disloyal to edit a book with another writer and not with him. I sent him about his business.

He then went to a publisher and arranged to do a rival book on Wordsworth.

I had a letter from Howard Sergeant, possibly about some poems, at a later time in the 'fifties. The writing paper made me shudder to think of what I had almost let myself in for. He had put on the letterhead his name in enormous type, followed by letters signifying various accountants' organizations he belonged to or was a fellow of, in a size at least five times that of a normal professional statement of qualifications on a letterhead. 'Letters after his name' were evidently his idea of glory.

Many years later still, when I had published many books, and enjoyed a lot of success with my novels, I met Howard Sergeant. He said he felt he had behaved badly towards me. I looked at him politely. I really could not like that man.

Of those last years of the 'forties Colin Methven remains a constantly sweet memory. After his daughter Deirdre's marriage I saw little of him. But Colin's affection for me was warm and steady and I felt the same towards him. I really needed that friendship amidst the madness and frenzy of the Poetry Society. I worried about his health. His heart trouble prevented him from coming to London except on rare occasions.

Many times during my ordeal at the Poetry Society Colin would send a special messenger with tickets for the theatre, for Ascot, for art exhibitions. I could rarely use them. I had an increasing work-load that kept me busy often until eleven at night, not the least of which was a massive and useless correspondence with individual Society members. A lot of time was spent not only defending my position, but also considering manuscripts, pasting up the final format, as we did in those days when sending a magazine to press. On those late nights I would have to take a taxi home, always at my own expense. Throughout all this Colin was an unfailing source of good humour and light. I only have to catch a glimpse of his handwriting among my papers and I feel a glow of happiness.

Two years after I had left the Poetry Society, the then Poet Laureate, John Masefield, said to me, 'All experience is good for an artist.' I have always believed this to be true.

I transferred a number of my experiences in the Poetry Society, as I usually do, into a fictional background, in my novel *Loitering With Intent*.

CHAPTER SEVEN

After leaving the Poetry Society I became aware of the value of documentary evidence, both as a means of personal defence against inaccuracies and as an aid to one's own memory. Consequently, since 1949 onwards I have thrown away practically nothing on paper. Almost every letter I have received, every note I have made, every cheque-book, every book of accounts, every appointments book, lists of names and addresses, my correspondence with publishers and agents throughout the world, with income tax departments, accountants, lawyers, turf accountants (I like racing when in England) – all and everything, I have conserved in a vast archive. The only, partial, exception are the letters of my friend and literary partner of the 'fifties, Derek Stanford. They arrived daily, so thick and fast, that I could not guard them all. Even so, more than five hundred of his letters survive.

After more than fifty years, this collection has amounted to a social history in itself. One thing I have always known about my well-ordered archive is that it would stand by me, the silent, objective evidence of truth, should I ever need it. It has given me the confidence to proceed calmly with my creative work during all these years when not a few rash writers, 'scholars' and journalists have made absurd and false statements about my life, based often on the faulty memory of one and copied in garbled form by the other. Supported, moreover, by the kindness of universities who have made available to me letters of mine which have been sold to them, I have always known that when the time came I could put the record straight wherever necessary. Scholars who have honoured me by writing books about my work, and students who choose my writings for their theses, can hardly be blamed for copying what they conceive to be 'facts' carelessly put about by the first 'spokesman'.

Amongst my papers, those five hundred-plus letters from Derek Stanford are an invaluable guide to my everyday life, my whereabouts on almost any given day or week, the dates on which I moved from one small bed-sitting-room to another, and the work I was absorbed in. The letters came nearly all from Derek's home at Hounslow, or occasionally from the Baldur Book Shop at Richmond where he had a part-time job. The letters also describe Derek's literary activities and friendships. Sometimes I failed to open these near-daily letters, being too busy, and so I found them, recently, after nearly half a century, still sealed. Derek Stanford's letters are full of his ailments, whether from hypochondria or from genuine illness, let us not split hairs. The fact is that phrases like 'The worst has happened. I am in bed with a cold' and 'My doctors say that I must avoid the night air' abound. It so happened that when I recently came upon one of Derek's unopened letters addressed to me so long ago, I said to the friend who was helping me to sort them: 'I bet it's about his health.' Sure enough, the note begins: 'The worst has come to pass, and here I am still in bed on Monday morning.' I tried another. It starts, 'Had such a bad stomach-turn yesterday that I must decline the pleasure of going with you on Sunday to June and Neville's' (i.e. my friends June and Neville Braybrooke). And the next: 'Unbelievable as it may seem, the worst has happened & I am down with *another* splendid cold & cough ... The sneezes are abated somewhat to-day but the chest ...'

Derek Stanford was a young critic and poet about my age. He was as different from the macho Howard Sergeant as could be imagined. Derek came from a respectable ordinary-class family. He was an only child and lived all the time I knew him with his parents at 46 Lulworth Avenue, Lampton, Hounslow. He was amusing, very eccentric, short, frail and almost totally bald. You could never imagine him on a dance floor or with a tennis racquet in his hand. He was bookish with scholarly leanings, but, as I found gradually, and later to my cost, wildly and almost constitutionally inaccurate.

From the first he was very keen to set up a literary partnership with me and I readily agreed. I found his company refreshing after Howard, and his love of literature infectious. Derek could not be bothered with man-woman jealousy. If I made or received a phone call in his presence, he never wanted to know, nor did he care who 'the man' was. This was civilized; I didn't take any notice, and rightly, when Derek wrote to tell me about his previous sexual hang-ups 'with men and women'. I felt his past was none of my business. I also felt his parents were none of my business, although he was extremely cagey about them – I never knew why. My own parents and Robin, I made available to everyone I knew. My mother liked Derek. She thought him out of the ordinary, 'a character'. My father had reservations about this friendship. When in the course of a few years it fizzled out, my father was relieved, understandably remembering my marriage with a man whose background we knew nothing about. And when, even later on, after my name had acquired some definite fame, and Derek sold the letters (about seventy in number) I had written to him which survived, my father remarked that 'the only decent thing that man did was not marry you'. By that time (in the 'sixties), I heartily agreed.

While on the subject of letters, I will take a leap forward to describe, now, the approach which was made to me about those letters I had written to Derek, how horrible it was.

Early in July 1963 an American dealer called Lew D. Feldman asked me if I had manuscripts and letters for sale. I said no, but when he pressed I let him come to my flat to 'value' the holograph manuscripts of my novels. I wrote to report to my lawyer, Michael Rubinstein, to tell him about that visit. Feldman wanted to take away all my papers in a taxi. Of course, I refused. He let drop that he had my letters to Derek Stanford, and might sell them back to me. I wrote to Michael Rubinstein: 'I am far too proud to think of buying them back – even if they were wild and terrible I wouldn't do so, and they are fairly mild.' When I saw photocopies quite recently I realized how true this was. These letters are fluent, affectionate, sexless. They deal mainly with publishers and payments for work, literature and religion. However, what made me anxious was Feldman's statement that he had 'other material'. I wrote to Rubinstein to report: 'When I pointed out that any writings of mine, apart from letters, . . . were stolen property, he said he quite saw this was a delicate point.' Delicate point!

Not long after this I became aware of the loss from my trunks of two treasured notebooks of juvenilia and some early stories. The poems were written out carefully in my schoolgirl hand – some of them were quite mature poems. I asked my mother, did she know where they had gone? She searched high and low. She went to my school-friend Frances (Niven) Cowell who also looked among her things to see if I had left them with her, long ago; but no luck. Only lately have I discovered that I brought those poems to London from Edinburgh in the spring of 1952, describing them in a letter to Derek Stanford. The poems have now turned up in the libraries of two separate universities in the US, sold to them with another pile of my manuscript material by Feldman. This is by no means the fault of the universities, who assumed that Feldman was a regular dealer. I do not care so much about letters, the physical copies of which are, by law, the property of the recipient although the copyrights are mine. But I dó care about my two stolen childhood notebooks. To me, they are family things. They are exactly what my son, my great-niece, or my great-nephews would appreciate to be left to them when I die. Instead, those notebooks of my young dreams went to

line the pockets of unscrupulous strangers. As Frances writes,
'It leaves a sore spot in the heart.'

I saw Feldman once more, in New York where I had gone to
write, later in 1963. He again offered me those letters I had
written to Stanford, now billed as 'embarrassing'. On the advice
of my lawyer I went along to Feldman's flat to look at these much-
vaunted letters. I took my agent and friend, Ivan von Auw, to
give me moral support. Feldman took out from a drawer the pile
of letters. (Of course, he did not show me my stolen manuscripts.) 'Fifteen hundred dollars,' said Feldman. It was horrible
seeing his fingers clutching those handwritten pages of my earlier
self, when I was so poor, so determined to face hardship in order
to succeed in literature, and at one point so very ill from under-
nourishment. I took the pages and flicked them through without
really reading them. Ivan had a sense of humour. 'With fifteen
hundred dollars she could go round the world,' he said.

It was true that fifteen hundred dollars was a large sum in
1963. But I wouldn't have bought back those letters at any price.
Going down in the lift to the street door Ivan and I both agreed
that we felt like having a bath. Instead Ivan took me for a lovely
lunch at the Pavillon on East 57th Street.

Derek Stanford's main fault as a critic was his inaccuracy. It
brought in a great many complaints. A book he wrote on
Christopher Fry was challenged publicly by Fry's friend,
Robert Gittings. I was so sorry for despondent Derek that I
wrote to Gittings a sort of defence, but I was on the losing side.
Robert Gittings pointed out that a silly dance-lyric had been
attributed to Fry, which in fact was not his work, and
recommended me to feel concern that Derek's published works
be accurate. It was often small facts, dates and titles that Derek
couldn't get right. He wrote an appreciation of Percy Lubbock in
The Month to celebrate the award to Lubbock of an 'OM' which,
Stanford pointed out, was far above a CBE. In fact it was a CBE

that Lubbock received. In a literary collaborator, this careless-
ness puzzled me and worried me in those early 'fifties.

When, in the 'sixties, I was already a well-established writer,
and after Stanford had sold my letters, I heard that he was to
write a book about me, I shuddered. I didn't feel ready yet for a
book to be written about me in any case, and wrote to the *Times
Literary Supplement* to express my feeling that the time was not
ripe.

When the book came out it was, of course, packed with factual
errors. These are some of the errors that scholars and students
have been taking as fact ever since. I felt Stanford's disregard for
truth very uncharitable towards students and scholars who had
put part of their life work into studying my writings, only to find,
having taken Stanford's word, that they had formed theories and
drawn conclusions from false premises. The *Times Literary
Supplement* reviewer (25 October 1963), for one, was of course
sceptical about much of what Stanford said. The reviewer wrote:

> Perhaps a writer who refers to Miss Spark taking a fortnight
> off to read through *Recherche dans le temps perdu* [*sic*] rather
> puts himself out of court as a critic of fiction . . .
> . . . He is keen to notice evidence of Miss Spark's 'delicate
> oral' [*sic*] sense, but, perhaps because he is clearly out of
> sympathy with her complex attitude towards the Church of
> her adoption, he sees her wit as merely verbal, when it surely
> springs from more savage and spiritual depth.

Stanford resented my success as a novelist. He always made out
that my narrative writing was a frivolous activity. (He endured,
in fact, a nervous breakdown at the time of my first success.)

Having got off his chest this book containing a large number of
inaccuracies, some of them merely foolish, about my personal
life and my family, Stanford was virtually lost from sight for
fourteen years. He surfaced again in 1977 with a book about the
'forties in which I feature prominently. His later memory,

untutored and unsupported by anything so trivial as evidence or documents, now flourished and ran wild. I give Derek Stanford full marks for bright colours. Some of his inventions are truly exotic. But people wishing to have my biographical details are wrongly induced by Stanford's self-styled spokesmanship to imagine that the few years in which Stanford was acquainted with me are the sum total of my life.

As an aid to scholars and students (I hereby beg them, in their own interests, to check with me before using any Stanford material that they are unable themselves to substantiate), I cite the following examples of sheer guesswork, mythomania, invention or what you will, on the part of Stanford:

He claims that my grandmother had gypsy blood. (I would challenge any genealogist to prove this picturesque proposition. Stanford bases his 'evidence' on the fact that one of my characters, Louisa Jepp, in my novel *The Comforters* is a half-gypsy.) He says that I went with him to visit an 'Uncle Solly' of mine, about money. (I have asked round the family who this could be. We have no uncle or cousin or grandfather or great-uncle Solly. And nobody by that or any other name who was especially rich. I can only think Stanford has confused me here with someone else.) He writes that I was suckled till I was two years old. (My mother's comment: 'How ridiculous! There must be something wrong with the man.') He says that I was in love with T.S. Eliot. (My comment: I never met Eliot. He was my parents' age. But if Stanford thought I was in love with another man, why was *he* hanging around?) He claims that I went to 'Eliot's church' in Gloucester Road. (Presumably Stanford wants to suggest that I was hanging around Eliot.) But I never went to any church in Gloucester Road. The church I attended until I became a Roman Catholic was, on the advice of the editor of the *Church of England Newspaper*, the nearest one to my home at 1 Queen's Gate Terrace, St Augustine's, Queen's Gate. Stanford asserts that he met Miss Kay, the origin of my character Miss Brodie. (No, Miss Kay died before I knew

Stanford. The teacher he met in London in 1949 was my senior English teacher, Alison Foster.)

It should not be assumed that by citing the few trivial examples above I accept the rest of Stanford's claims as accurate. I could go on for pages. I would write off almost the lot as examples of fabulism, or an inadequate sense of objectivity.

But those efforts of Stanford do not have a pleasant tone. They contain a touch of the sniggering schoolboy, or of the gossip-columnist, that only scholars of equal leanings would seize on and elaborate. His attitude to me after my success was totally unmerited. Our friendship had long since fizzled out. But I had treated him generously, as had my family.

I owed him thanks for the fact that during an illness of mine he acted as intermediary between me and the world, and obtained for me enough money from well-wishers, notably Graham Greene, to be able to recuperate.

But Stanford's writings about me, with their cheap overtones, did him more harm than good. His book on the 'forties raised a volley of protests from other people whom he had described wrongly. I was too busy to raise my voice at the time. I said nothing then. I have said it now, this being the place.

To return to the 'fifties: emerging from the Poetry Society I had found to my surprise that my name had become known and that I was fairly popular with the press, on account of my editorial taste. But I had not yet earned a literary reputation by my own writing. And reputation apart I had a love of writing which was becoming an imperative in my life. With an idea developing in my head, a pen in my hand and a notebook open before me I was in bliss.

To keep myself going I had a part-time job in the very lively offices of *European Affairs*. This was a magazine for and about Eastern Europe and its exiles. It was run by Elma Dangerfield, a clever English society woman, and Monty Radulovitch, a

Montenegrin journalist who had written a book on Tito. Our offices were often full of members of shadow cabinets and vociferous exiles from Poland, Rumania, Russia, huddled always in their overcoats.

I would have involved myself far more in this exotic enterprise had I not vowed to give my main attention to my literary work. I was with *European Affairs* full time for a while, and then I had to explain that I could only do three days a week. Monty Radulovitch accepted this offer although Elma Dangerfield, his partner, was against it. She was a creature of the 'thirties, petite, with a short, tight, head-hugging coiffure and short, tight, body-hugging dresses. I kept an ear out for her voice and her terms of expression, as I always do with people. Monty's way of speech was a treasure-house to me. I was not yet writing stories and novels, but I was working towards the narrative art, and saved up 'voices' in my memory-file. The phrase of Monty's that I remember most was the warning: 'Elma, you regret thees, you regret thees, Elma, all your life.' So it was when Elma wanted to refuse my offer of three days' work a week. 'Elma, you regret thees.' Elma gave in and I stayed. I always had a soft spot for Monty, and in later years when he was on his own and had to put his thoughts into good English I would type out his letters and press-releases on a friendly basis.

I was now living at No. 1, Vicarage Gate, a short way up Kensington Church Street from Kensington High Street. The name of this rooming house was Eras House. I had a small single-bed room, a gas ring and a wash basin. This is largely the scene of my novel *Loitering With Intent*. Not far away was St Mary Abbot's church and extended churchyard which has now long since been made over as a playground. But in those days of the early 'fifties the old Victorian graves were still standing, overgrown with weeds, with the names and strange dedicatory epitaphs still visible. I used to take my sandwich lunch there on fine days, when I had my days off, and write my poems. Always, now, on my desk, was the book I was writing.

193

My first project with Derek Stanford was to edit a book on Wordsworth to mark the centenary of his death in 1850. Derek had published a book of poems and one of criticism, but I was new to the publishing of books. We found a sympathetic publisher in André Deutsch, then of Allan Wingate, who impressed me very much by his intelligence and courtesy. He went out of his way for us as if we were world-famous authors intead of small-time beginners. In fact André Deutsch, my first publisher, was one of the nicest I have ever met.

The book was divided into two parts: Derek took care of the nineteenth-century critics from whom he published extracts while I wrote to the younger critics to get essays from them. The earlier part of the twentieth century I covered in my introduction. The book also had a joint introduction by us both. I remember deciding at that stage that if I were to edit or write any more joint productions in prose with anybody we would each have to contribute our separate part. Word by word composition was agonizing to me. Derek's prose was flamboyant and convoluted; mine, simple. Apart from that reservation, when I look now at *Tribute to Wordsworth* as we called it, I feel genuinely that it was an excellent handbook for students. Derek's section was by far the richer, for most of the nineteenth-century essays he reprinted were out of copyright, whereas the contemporary writers had to be paid by the publisher's modest budget. Derek and I earned twenty-five pounds each for this book. My gross literary earnings for 1949 totalled one hundred and twenty-nine pounds, five shillings. This included payment for the Wordsworth book and some reviews and poems in various magazines. My part-time job made up the meagre rest.

My next literary work written in 1950 was entirely my own, a full-length study of Mary Shelley which I published in 1951 with a small publisher, Pen-in-Hand (later Tower Bridge Publications). To get myself started on this big task I gave up my part-time job, although I sometimes continued to write articles for *European Affairs* on a free-lance basis. H.K. Grant, the former Librarian of the Poetry Society, helped me a great deal, in a spirit of pure devotion (for he wanted no reward) by looking up and copying information that I needed from the British Museum, or acquiring the necessary books from local free libraries. *Child of Light* was my title for this book (which more recently I have revised under the title *Mary Shelley*). Writing against time for economic reasons and at the same time trying to be scrupulously accurate was not easy. I often sat up writing far into the night. A poet-friend, Iris Birtwistle, had generously given me a typewriter but I used this only for the final draft (which had to be done by day so as not to disturb the other tenants of the rooming-house). That year, 1950, my gross literary earnings were one hundred and thirty-four pounds, three shillings and threepence, but by the time my book was published in 1951 I had taken another part-time job with a public relations man, Pearson Horder. My job was actually to write speeches for industrialists based on very few data, sometimes merely the contents of the firm's hand-out brochures. I remember one of my speeches about manager-employee relationships being particularly successful. How did I manage it? I really don't know. I think I must have parodied everything I had dimly heard or read on the subject, racked around in my imagination, and then thrown in a bit of existential philosophy to make it sound impressive. How I wish I had a copy of that speech now! I can't even remember which industrialist was to deliver the speech. I recall a Mr Colston of Hoover Washing Machines as one of Horder's clients, but whether that particular speech was intended for him or for another, I can't now say.

The public relations job really wore my heart away. I would look out of the window and think of Paul Verlaine's lines from prison:

> *Le ciel est, par-dessus le toit,*
> *Si bleu, si calme!*

and long for the hours to pass so that I could walk home through the park.

But my *Child of Light* had some favourable reviews. I had already gone to see Alan Pryce-Jones who was then editor of the *Times Literary Supplement*. To my great pleasure he commissioned me to write a middle page on Mary Shelley, which appeared before publication. I remember Derek Stanford was rather taken aback by this, and rather too immediately wrote off to Alan Pryce-Jones asking for work for himself without success. I felt rather embarrassed about this, but Derek had generally, with my permission, used my address when writing to publishers about his own affairs as well as about our joint productions. We sometimes translated or wrote poems together, each doing a different verse. An address in Kensington was much better for Derek, especially in those days, than one in Hounslow where he lived.

P.H. Newby, head of the Third Programme at the BBC, next commissioned me to give a talk on Mary Shelley. I was rapidly becoming better known. I edited, with Derek, a selection of Mary Shelley's letters. The introduction, this time, was done in the form of dialogue, I writing my paragraph and Derek replying in his own words. It was a much better system.

Sometimes, on free days, I would go for a walk in the country with Derek. St Albans was our favourite spot. It was near to London and I remembered so well the woods and lanes of my childhood holidays in Hertfordshire.

That year, 1951, I continued to write a flow of articles and poems, and I got together my first book of poetry, *The Fanfarlo and Other Verse*, which was published in 1952 by Erica Marx. Erica, a dear friend, was the owner of the Hand and Flower Press. She was fairly well off and her series of poetry books was financed entirely out of her own pocket. She published good poets, mainly at a loss. (She was amused to note that she actually made a profit, much later when I had an established name, out of my *Fanfarlo*.)

Wrey Gardiner, who was a director of Grey Walls Press, now commissioned me to edit a selection of Emily Brontë's poems in their famous Crown Classics series. I did this, but had to wait for a long, long time for my money.

That year, I started writing my book on the works of John Masefield. I had now moved to 65 Old Brompton Road, to a furnished room in the flat of Mr and Mrs Andipatin, a fine couple from Mauritius. From there I had written the previous winter to Masefield and was asked to come and see him at Burcote Brook, near Oxford. I went on a freezing day, Wednesday, 6 December 1950. It was a thrilling visit, to a poet I much admired. I was now moving, myself, from lyric poetry to narrative verse. This was the start of my move in literature towards the short story and then the novel. I took a passionate interest in Arthur Hugh Clough's novel in verse *Amours de Voyage*, about which I am still enthusiastic. And I felt that Masefield's stories in verse, *Reynard the Fox* and *Dauber*, were shamefully neglected. I have recently revised and republished my book, *John Masefield*. In the new introduction is a long portion of my journal entry describing my visit, his marvellous conversation, and especially his personal reminiscences of Swinburne. Although I found his house rather cold – we each had a small paraffin stove by our chair at lunch – and there was no alcoholic drink, it was one of the happiest days of my life. I remember well the euphoria of the white, frozen landscape around the house. It was on this occasion that Masefield spoke those words that I was to remember later: 'All experience is good for an artist.'

On the way to the station after lunch I dived into a pub next to Blackwell's in Broad Street and put back a double rum.

I spent 1951 writing my book on John Masefield. I had a new part-time survival-job at Falcon Press where I was secretary to a charming retired major, Walter Meade. Much of this environment goes into my novel, *A Far Cry from Kensington*. Walter wrote very good poetry. He had written the screenplay of *Scott of the Antarctic.* He had been sent into the firm by the owner's father, Reginald Baker, who was an Ealing Studio tycoon. But even Baker's money could not eventually save his son Peter, a reckless spender and forger, from an over-harsh seven-year prison sentence. In the period of my work at Falcon Press, however, Peter was still flourishing.

In that year 1951 came the first real turning-point in my career. In November *The Observer* announced a short-story competition on the subject of Christmas. The first prize was two hundred and fifty pounds, quite a fortune in those days, with various secondary prizes.

The rules were that the story should be not more than three thousand words, and the entry should be anonymous. The story was to be accompanied by an envelope signed by a pseudonym on the outside, the real name inside.

I put aside my work on Masefield and wrote 'The Seraph and the Zambesi' on foolscap paper, straight off. Now I had to type it but I found I had no typing paper. I scrounged some from the owner of an art shop nearby in South Kensington, typed it out, put my pseudonym 'Aquarius' on the envelope and my name and address inside, and mailed it all off to *The Observer* that afternoon.

I used to keep a notebook which I called my 'Despatch Book'. This is still among my papers. On the right side of the page I wrote the name of the journal to which I submitted my work as I wrote it. On the left I wrote against it, when the fate of the submitted piece was known, either the words 'accepted' or 'returned' – more often than not the latter. I see on one page that I sent a poem called 'The Messengers' to the *Times Literary Supplement* on 28 October (returned); and on the same day a poem 'The Nativity' to *Time and Tide* (returned). On 29 October I sent a poem 'Hymn to Apollo' to *The Listener* (returned). On 1 November I sent a parody verse-play *The Cocktail's Not for Drinking* to *Adelphi* (returned), and on 1 November a poem 'The Conversation of the Angels' (returned). On 5 November I recorded '*The Observer Short Story Comp., The Seraph, the Zambesi, and the Fanfarlo.*' This time my comment on the left-hand side of the page is 'Got it'. For, near Christmas, I had a phone call from Philip Toynbee of *The Observer*. My story had won first place out of six thousand seven hundred entries. 'We thought it was written by a man until we opened the envelope,' said Philip. I don't know if I was supposed to be flattered by that.

The story was published on the following Sunday. I had by now met and liked the *Observer* editor and staff. The editor, David Astor, Philip Toynbee and Terence Kilmartin had been the judges. Just after midnight on the Sunday of publication, David Astor himself brought the paper to me. It was thrilling to have the newspaper delivered by the editor.

Derek Stanford had not been keen on my wasting my time on story-writing, but now to make him happy I gave him fifty pounds for Christmas. My son, who to my parents' satisfaction had decided to be a Jew, also got fifty pounds to pay for a party for his bar mitzvah. I bought myself a blue velvet dress for six pounds and a complete set of Proust's *A la Recherche du Temps Perdu.*

I took Derek to introduce him to some *Observer* editors at their local pub. This wasn't a great success. Philip Toynbee wore a detachable dog-collar. (Philip claimed that he had found it agreeable during the war, as a young officer, to get into a first-class carriage on a train, wearing his clerical collar, and lecture colonels and generals about their morals.) Derek, on this occasion, said to Philip, 'I did not know you had taken orders, Mr Toynbee.' Whereupon Philip took off his collar and drank his beer in a long draught. He definitely did not take to Derek who had begun to display ever more eighteenth-century affectations.

My story caused quite a stir.

Not long after this, in January 1952, Tony Strachan, who was to become a lifelong friend, came to join us at Falcon Press. Tony was already a novelist. Walter Meade interviewed Tony, and when he had gone said, 'What a nice young man.' Tony got a job with us. He reminisces how 'the only real pro in the firm, Alex Fulcher, the traveller,' greeted him: '"What the hell do you want to come and work here for? Baker's a madman."' Fulcher offered Tony seven pounds a week. 'Peter Baker came in and said, "I was thinking of more like six pounds ten."' Tony also reminds me about the bad-debts sheriff's officer or bailiff who was 'so constantly in attendance that when he died there was some confusion as to whether or not he was a member of the staff, who clubbed together to buy him a wreath.'

'No one', writes Tony Strachan, 'has ever been as poor as you were in those days. I mean someone of education, culture and background. You told Billie [Tony's wife] that you had one dress, and your shoes had holes in them.'

This was true. I was getting tired of it. I also had very little to eat. Those were days of rationing, tighter even than during the war. If one didn't eat the whole of the allotted rations one was in trouble. In 1952 to 1953 a single person was allowed one and a half ounces of cheese, four ounces of bacon, two eggs and eight ounces of butter per week (there was a special coronation issue of four ounces of butter in May 1953). Butcher's meat was rationed by price, limited to one shilling and ninepence per week in 1953. This was, in fact, the basis of a fairly balanced minimum diet. But living alone, as I did, I neglected to take these basics. I didn't care enough. Derek, whose ration book was naturally registered at home together with those of his parents and whose rations were collected by them, used to visit me about twice a week and of course automatically share my meagre rations. I don't imagine for a moment that he thought of rations or of food. In all the great mass of letters he wrote to me he never mentioned food. Neither did I, but the fact remains that I was thoroughly undernourished. When I went to Edinburgh for *The Observer* to cover the Edinburgh Festival in 1953 I felt thoroughly ill, and hardly knew what I was doing.

Tony Strachan had always begged me to give up working on

literary criticism and biographies. I was now editing a book of the Brontë letters which in fact I think was successful. I made it deliberately read like a story. Jointly with Derek I planned a book on Emily Brontë. I was responsible for the biographical section, he, the critical. This essay on Emily Brontë is, I believe, my most closely reasoned piece of non-fictional prose. But Tony was right. He positively nagged me about the waste of my talent, and in fact, only a few years later, it was Tony Strachan who persuaded Macmillan and their editor, Alan Maclean, to commission a novel from me.

One day in 1953, a lunch was given at the Ritz for writers on the Shelleys by the famous Shelley collector Carl H. Pforzheimer and his wife. As the author of a book on Mary Shelley I was invited. It was 24 July 1953. There I had red caviare for the first time in my life. The party included a number of Shelley scholars, notably the poets Cecil Day Lewis and Edmund Blunden. Day Lewis was enchanted by the two very pretty young Pforzheimer granddaughters who were on their way to do the Grand Tour of Europe with their grandparents. Mr Pforzheimer made an interesting speech, followed by Cecil Day Lewis and then by Edmund Blunden. I recall talking to a man on my right and exchanging addresses with him – I took my little diary out of my bag, then put it back again. I also remember – but only after nearly forty years – that as I put my handbag down on the floor on my left side, Edmund Blunden, sitting on my left, fished into it and took my notebook out. I thought this was a bit of foolery and was too champagned-up to really notice. Only recently, checking on the date of that lovely Pforzheimer lunch, I came across an entry written by another hand than mine underneath the date 24 July 1953 and my own note 'Pforzheimer Shelley lunch'. The words are: 'This is a reminder that you were at this lunch and endured a speech by E. Blunden. Please come to Charing X Sta. on 4 Aug at 6 p.m.'

I didn't read that message of Blunden's until 1991 – rather too late to keep the date. I doubt if he really expected me to do so.

Sometimes one particular day in its entirety is vivid in one's memory. On the way home from that Pforzheimer lunch I bumped into Father Philip Caraman, a 'Farm Street' Jesuit, editor of *The Month*. Philip Caraman was a much-loved friend of a great many writers, known and unknown, Catholic and otherwise. Philip said if I would walk back with him to the office he would give me a book to review. On the way there, I felt in the mood to entertain him with some amusing stories. He gave me the book to review and a cheque for fifteen pounds for having made him laugh.

In 1953 I was absorbed by the theological writings of John Henry Newman through whose influence I finally became a Roman Catholic. I tried the Church of England first, as being more 'natural' and near to home. But I felt uneasy. It was historically too new for me to take to. When I am asked about my conversion, why I became a Catholic, I can only say that the answer is both too easy and too difficult. The simple explanation is that I felt the Roman Catholic faith corresponded to what I had always felt and known and believed; there was no blinding revelation in my case. The more difficult explanation would involve the step by step building up of a conviction; as Newman himself pointed out, when asked about his conversion, it was not a thing one could propound 'between the soup and the fish' at a dinner party. 'Let them be to the trouble that I have been to,' said Newman. Indeed, the existential quality of a religious experience cannot be simply summed up in general terms.

With Derek Stanford I later edited a selection of Cardinal Newman's letters. Derek took charge of the Anglican letters and I those of his Catholic years. To help me, Philip Caraman lent me a bundle of Newman's original letters to various Jesuits. I had them with me all the time I was working on the book. I found it good to touch the very papers that the sublime Father Newman had touched.

On 1 May 1954 I was received into the Church at Ealing

Priory by the late Dom Ambrose Agius, a warm and kindly Maltese priest whom I had met at the Poetry Society. I had a great many Catholic friends; I suppose one is naturally drawn to others of like beliefs. My sponsors when I was received were June and Neville Braybrooke, both very good writers, who lived at Hampstead. June wrote exquisite novels under the name of Isobel English. I loved to visit them; they were brimming with intelligence and wit. Christine Brooke-Rose was then married to Jerzy Pietrkiewicz, a Polish writer, fluent in English. I had a close friendship with them. Both were academics, and both had written highly interesting novels.

The non-Catholics of my close acquaintance were always willing to discuss theology, especially when it touched on a subject very important to me, the Book of Job. It seemed to me that the Comforters in Job were not at all distinct characters; they were very much of one type. They were, in fact, like modern interrogators who come to interview and mock the victim in shifts. I was to express part of this theory and conviction years later, in my novel, *The Only Problem*. My first novel, which I called *The Comforters* (a title I came to after much trial and error), describes the persecuting effect of the 'voices' experienced by the main character. As a title it is perhaps not precise enough.

In 1953 on my return from Edinburgh, feeling desperately weak, I wrote a review, in the *Church of England Newspaper*, of T.S. Eliot's play *The Confidential Clerk* which was first performed at the Edinburgh Festival. The editor, the Rev. Clifford Rhodes, sent the review to Eliot, who replied to him, very favourably, on 30 September. Clifford Rhodes passed on Eliot's reply to me. He thanked Rhodes for the critique of his play by me, and added:

I should have acknowledged it as soon as I read it, for it struck me as one of the two or three most intelligent reviews I had read. It seemed to me remarkable that anyone who could only have seen the play once, and certainly not have read it, should have grasped so much of its intention.

This, of course, made me feel very cheerful. I was already embarked on a study of Eliot. Frank Sheed of Sheed & Ward commissioned a short book.

So I continued my Eliot studies. But in 1954 shortly after my reception into the Church of Rome something strange occurred. Something strange was not surprising, because, foolishly, I had been taking dexedrine as an appetite suppressant, so that I would feel less hungry. It was a mad idea.

As I worked on the Eliot book one night the letters of the words I was reading became confused. They formed anagrams and crosswords. In a way, as long as this sensation lasted, I knew they were hallucinations. But I didn't connect them with the dexedrine. It is difficult to convey how absolutely fascinating that involuntary word-game was. I thought at first that there was a code built into Eliot's work and tried to decipher it. Next, I seemed to realize that this word-game went through other books by other authors. It appeared that they were phonetics of Greek, and were extracts from the Greek dramatists.

This experience lasted from 25 January to 22 April 1954. I saw Dr Lieber, a general practitioner, in Wimpole Street. Dr Lieber was an old friend, a private – that is to say, not a National Health – doctor. He agreed to treat me without fees until I was better again. But he explained that lots of women in those days of rationing gave up part of their share to their families, and consequently suffered from under-nourishment. I know he suspected that I ate the wrong food for while I was convalescent in the country he wrote to me frequently; I still have his letters. 'Be sure to eat the right food,' he says repeatedly.

My friends, June and Neville, Christine and Jerzy, were very sympathetic. I was aware of being surrounded by friends. Matter-of-fact Hugo Manning, a night-journalist who worked on Reuters, and also a poet and amateur philosopher, was a great source of moral support. As soon as I stopped taking dexedrine the delusions of the word-game stopped. But I felt ill, as I had felt at Edinburgh the previous year. I found a friend in Father Frank O'Malley, a kind of lay-psychologist and Jungian. He didn't think I needed to go for psychiatric treatment, but I saw him often. In the mean time Graham Greene, through Derek Stanford, had offered to give me a monthly sum of twenty pounds until I got better. He really admired my work and was enthusiastic about helping me. With the cheque he would often send a few bottles of red wine – as I was happy to record when speaking at Graham's memorial service – which took the edge off cold charity.

I took refuge first at Aylesford in Kent at the Carmelite monastery, and next at nearby Allington Castle, near Maidstone, a Carmelite stronghold of tertiary nuns. There I rented a cottage in the grounds, and it was there that I put into effect the determination I had fixed upon, to write a novel about my recent brief but extremely intense word-game experience.

It so happened that in 1954, in the crucial months of my illness, my name was beginning to flourish in the literary world. It was in a way frustrating that I was unable to respond positively to so many letters from publishers, magazines and universities who were writing to me then for stories, reviews, lectures. One letter was particularly tempting. It came from Alan Maclean, the fiction editor of Macmillan, London, a much larger publisher than any I had so far dealt with. Alan Maclean, who was the best-liked editor in London, asked me to write a novel for his firm; they would commission it (a thing unheard of, for first novels, in those days). Alan had been urged to look for new young talent, and got my address from Tony Strachan, who was then working at Macmillan.

Feeling weak, as I did, I replied that I didn't write novels, only stories.

Back came a charming letter. A book of stories would be very acceptable. Was I interested? I think I said, yes, but I would need time to put a collection together.

After I was settled at Allington I began to think how I could go about writing a novel, and especially the novel about my hallucinations that I had resolved to write. I didn't feel like 'a novelist' and before I could square it with my literary conscience to write a novel, I had to work out a novel-writing process peculiar to myself, and moreover, perform this act within the very novel I proposed to write. I felt, too, that the novel as an art form was essentially a variation of a poem. I was convinced that any good novel, or indeed any composition which called for a constructional sense, was essentially an extension of poetry. It is always comforting to come across a confirmation of one's private feelings in the pronouncements of others who are more qualified to speak. I was particularly delighted when I came across the following piece of dialogue in a book of dialogue-criticism (*Invitation to Learning*, New York, 1942) mainly by the American scholars and writers, Huntington Cairns, Allen Tate (soon to be one of my closest friends) and Mark van Doren.

The magic piece of dialogue (they are discussing Bunyan's *The Pilgrim's Progress*) goes thus:

Van Doren: Why should we not say that this is trying to be a poem too? Any book that is trying to be good is trying to be a poem.

Tate: It is a poem because it deals with action conveyed through fictions of the imagination.

Van Doren: This would satisfy Aristotle's definition of a poem.

All my hallucinatory experiences, looking back on them, seemed to integrate with this idea. I always tell students of my work, and interviewers, that I think of myself as predominantly a poet.

From the aspect of method, I could see that to create a

character who suffered from verbal illusions on the printed page would be clumsy. So I made my main character 'hear' a typewriter with voices composing the novel itself. This novel, *The Comforters*, was published in February 1957. It was connected with a very curious literary coincidence that in fact turned out well in my favour.

Evelyn Waugh was, in the year 1954–55, someone quite outside of my orbit. But it happened that he, too, had been taking the wrong sort of pills precisely in 1954, and had suffered hallucinations, and had decided to write a novel about the experience. In his case, as most of his friends knew, he really did 'hear' voices. *The Ordeal of Gilbert Pinfold* was the result, published in the summer of 1957.

He wrote in a letter:

Mr Pinfold's experiences were almost exactly my own. I heard 'voices' such as I describe almost continuously day and night.

My novel was finished late in 1955. But before it was published there was a delay of a year, 1956. In the course of that year the proofs went round among literary people, one of whom was Gabriel Fielding, a very good novelist; his real name was Alan Barnsley, a medical doctor, practising in Maidstone. He knew about my illness but I believe he did not know about Waugh's. He was, however, in touch with Waugh on some business, and in the course of correspondence Alan Barnsley sent Evelyn Waugh the proofs of my first novel.

Waugh replied that 'the mechanics of the hallucinations are well managed. These particularly interested me as I am myself engaged on a similar subject.' To his friend, Ann Fleming, he wrote

I have been sent proofs of a very clever first novel by a lady named Muriel Spark. The theme is a Catholic novelist suffering from hallucinations. It will appear quite soon. I am sure people will think it is by me. Please contradict such assertions.

On publication of my novel Evelyn Waugh was extremely generous, writing a most interesting essay on it in the *Spectator*.

Recently I asked Evelyn Waugh's eldest son, Auberon (Bron) if he remembers his father's reaction on getting those proofs of *The Comforters* while in the middle of writing his *Pinfold*.

All I remember [wrote Bron in reply] is him singing the praises of it, and saying how curious it was that you should be writing about the same sort of experience at the same time.

His attack, of course, was brought on by a mixture of chloral and bromide, yours by dexedrine, which should have the opposite effect to chloral and bromide. The sentence which jumps out from Evelyn Waugh's review is surely: 'It so happens that *The Comforters* came to me just as I had finished a story on a similar theme, and I was struck by how much more ambitious was Miss Spark's essay and how much better she had accomplished it.'

In the middle of 1955, before I had finished my first novel, I moved back to London, fully restored and brimming with plans. By the end of the year I had a book of short stories *The Go-Away Bird* ready for the publisher, and early in 1956 I started my second novel, *Robinson*.

The year 1956 was still very difficult financially. The long delay in publishing my first novel was due to Macmillan's getting cold feet about it. That novel was thought to be difficult, especially in those days – for it is true that one forms and 'educates' one's own public. Readers of novels were not yet used to the likes of me, and some will never be. But with Evelyn Waugh's first response and those of others who had seen the proofs, Macmillan took courage.

My digs in London were now 13 Baldwin Crescent, Camberwell, in a less fashionable part than in my old Kensington haunts. I had brought with me from the country a beautiful half-Persian stray cat, Bluebell, about whom I have written in poetry and prose. She was an extraordinary animal; I loved her dearly.

Father O'Malley and his cousin Teresa Walshe had found the place for me. The house was owned by Mrs Lazzari (Tiny), a wonderful Irish widow who had been married to an Italian cellist ('so I understand the Artist'). I stayed with Tiny for years and years. She was then about sixty. Right from the start, Tiny took me under her wing, encouraged me in my literary work, discouraged the hangers-on ('You're a bad picker' was her judgement of my choice of men-friends – how true!), and fed me her well-cooked meals for a very modest fee. Once, when I was depressed, Tiny made me pack my bags and accompany her 'home' to Cork, where we received a royal welcome from her daughter and their family.

Once, in a later and more prosperous year when I found Tiny heaving a scuttleful of coal for her fire from the cellar, and noticed how tired she looked, I said, 'Tiny, let's go to Paris tomorrow.' Tiny put down her coal. 'Okay,' she said. She had never been abroad before. On that occasion, while I was seeing my agent, Tiny wandered off by herself; she came back bringing with her for lunch my friend, Joe McCrindle, owner and editor of *Transatlantic Review*, who had visited at Baldwin Crescent. 'I bumped into Joe,' Tiny said, airily, as if the rue du Cherche-Midi was somewhere off Oxford Street.

While waiting for my novel to appear, I worked part time at Peter Owen the publisher. I liked the atmosphere a lot. Peter was a young publisher who was interested in books by Cocteau, Hermann Hesse, Cesare Pavese. It was a joy to proof-read the translations of such writers. I was secretary, proof-reader, editor, publicity girl; Mrs Bool was secretary, office manager and filing clerk; and Erna Horne, a rather myopic thick-lensed German refugee, was the book keeper. We were very attached to each other, there in the office at 50 Old Brompton Road, with one light bulb, bare boards on the floor, a long table which was the packing department, and Peter always retreating to his own tiny office to take phone calls from his uncles; one of them worked at Zwemmer the booksellers and gave us intellectual advice, and the other was a psychiatrist.

I worked at Peter Owen's three days a week, and at home wrote stories and my second novel, a kind of adventure story, *Robinson*.

At the beginning of 1957 when *The Comforters* was finally published, everything changed. Derek Stanford was still an occasional visitor at 13 Baldwin Crescent, but he was very unwell in those years. He was heading for a nervous breakdown.

My years of hardship and dedication were now bearing fruit, but my mounting success was an irritant to Derek's condition. There was nothing I could do about that. I tried to help by arranging with Macmillan to commission a new partnership-book by us both. They had paid an advance, which we shared. It was a second book on Cardinal Newman. But Derek had to give up the idea. His nervous state was acute. I had in fact felt rather under a strain as I was in a very awkward position. I readily allowed Derek's advance on the book to be deducted from my Macmillan royalties. But I could hardly keep my name out of the papers. At Stanford's request and to his expressed gratitude I wrote to Father O'Malley, who replied that he would see him. 'It would seem that this has been going on for some time,' he wrote. Plainly Fr. O'Malley felt it better for Derek to have professional help. The good priest sent him to Dr Elkesch and from there he was passed to the psychiatric department of Middlesex Hospital where he had treatment from a psychiatrist. To know that Derek was in safe professional hands was an enormous relief to me. He had been supportive throughout my illness, even to the point of packing up my papers and belongings in London for me when I went to recuperate in the country, and I wanted to be as considerate as possible. Derek wrote to me that he was advised not to see me; it made him ill. One evening when I was with a barrister friend, Tony (later Justice) Lincoln, waiting on the pavement for a cab, we had encountered Derek with some of his friends. This apparently – the meeting with me, not Tony Lincoln – upset Derek so much that he had to write to me about it. But I could hardly keep off the streets of London in order to avoid him. I wrote sympathetically, wishing him well. Later, Derek wrote to say he was going to marry an American girl named Delilah. Again, I wrote to wish him happiness. Whether he got married to Delilah or not I do not know. I lost sight of him after that and only heard of him when he wrote those shaky 'memoirs' of me.

But truly, I had now started a new life. Soon after publication of my novel in England Alan Maclean had found for me an American publisher, Lippincott. I was now able to give up my job with Peter Owen and write creatively, full time. '*The Comforters*', wrote Lippincott in May 1957, 'has caused a very agreeable stir among all of us who have read it.' That is exactly the sort of thing a first novelist wants to hear from a publisher. In March, *The New Yorker* wrote that they had admired my story 'The Portobello Road' which had appeared in Macmillan's *Winter's Tales*. They wondered 'if you won't let us consider some of your stories for publication.' This started my long and rewarding association with the magazine that is still considered the best in the world. Twice they have given up the whole of a week's issue to publish one of my novels in its entirety.

Financial stability took a long time to achieve, but I was no more anxious about the next week's rent, and was able to visit Edinburgh more often and eventually, New York. My mother was delighted, excited; my father smiled to himself with contentment. While I was away, Tiny could always be depended upon to keep me informed of what was going on. She had infinite courage. I have a letter in which she tells me in her own simple yet extremely expressive words about the death of her son, Bunny, which we had, sadly, expected. But added to this, she gives a full account of the daily occurrences at Baldwin Crescent.

She was really a remarkable friend. Here is her letter, verbatim:

My Dear Muriel,
At last I have got courage to break the news to you, I didnt
want to write untill you finished your novel, I cant keep it any
longer from you. I dont want to see any one else die with
cancer it is a very cruel thing God keep it from us, all the family
were here Joss came and she is looking very well, Charlie is
only just gone back I am on my own again I am glad in a way I
can get something done. Well dear the express [*Daily Express*]
rang yesterday and wanted to know where you were of course I
told them they wanted to know if you went for meterial for a
new Novel I said you had plenty of that without going away
just a business trip I do hope I was right. Everything is very
good here Charlie cleaned all your carpets they look very nice.
I am going home for Christmas I will be leaving here on 20th
of December ... well darling I miss you very much and I do
hope everything goes well for you I am always thinking of you
and wondering if you sleep and eate plenty do look after your
self
      I just feel I am going to hear something very good about you
God bless you
                                                All my love Tiny.

Tiny was a woman of considerable good looks. She always had
a fresh, neat and charming appearance. But she had an old-
fashioned widow's modesty. Once, in the course of a conversation with our neighbour, Mr Jackson, an odd-job man, when
we were discussing the merits and demerits of a certain type of
roof-gutter, Mr Jackson invited Tiny to step across the street to
inspect a neighbouring gutter which he had arranged for.

Tiny refused. Sensing that she had her own good reasons, I
kept silent. But after Mr Jackson had left, Tiny confided to me: 'I
wouldn't be seen crossing the street with a man. You never know
what people would say.'

Evelyn Waugh once wrote to me to say that now I was becoming established I should move to a good address. On paper, the advice was of course very wise. But nothing would part me from Tiny Lazzari and my rooms at 13 Baldwin Crescent where I could look over the peaceful back gardens and work so well.

I could never fully depict Tiny Lazzari. But I have done so partially in my novel *A Far Cry from Kensington*. She was a great deal of fun. Her energy was still superb when I last saw her. She was then ninety-four, quick-minded and positive. She died four years later, peacefully, of old age.

Since I wrote my first novel I have passed the years occupied with ever more work, many travels and adventures. Friends, famous and obscure, abound in my life-story. That will be the subject of another volume.

My story, as I have told it here, happened a long time ago, but the events are still strong in my mind. Especially I remember the sheer amusement of that day in February, on the publication of *The Comforters*, when not only Evelyn Waugh's essay in the *Spectator*, but the reviews in the other papers caused my editor Alan Maclean to ring me up at Peter Owen's office. 'You've hit the jackpot today,' said Al (as he was known to me).

Al took me to lunch the next week to a smart restaurant, Le Caprice, to celebrate. He had a bunch of reviews in his hand. 'I dare say', drawled Al, 'that this is the shape of things to come.' It was a risky saying, for many fine first novels are followed by duds. However, I took great heart from what he said, and went on my way rejoicing.

JUNE 5, 1993